An Entrepreneur's Journey in Pre - Liberal India

Arindam Dutta

ISBN:1484128028
ISBN-13:9781484128022

FOREWORD

My grandfather Shri Ramesh Chandra Roy Chowdhury (1890-70) was a chemist by training, a teacher (Jaggannath College, Dacca) by profession and a first generation entrepreneur by choice. He established the Laxminarayan Cotton Mills Ltd. at Narayangunj, in today's Bangladesh, and at Rishra, near Kolkata, India. The shares of the company were listed on both the Bombay and Kolkata Stock Exchanges. I had the opportunity to discuss with him over the years, as to how he was successful in doing what he did - the finance, the technology, the trained manpower needed, and most of all, sourcing raw materials from distant Gujarat[1]. As a teenager, I would sit with him and try and assimilate all that he was saying. It seems

[1] While at school, we read of the Bengal famine, the absolute deprivation of rural folk, and the pitiable infra-structure in the country side. Establishing a major spinning and weaving mills sounded so very discordant. My convent school training made it sound unbelievable.

that before independence, the center of Business – the so called Commercial Capital – was not Bombay, but Karachi. It all seemed like a Cinderella story.

But life is not a fairy tale. In 1965, during the Indo-Pak war, the mill at Narayangunj was acquired by the government of Pakistan under the Enemy Property Act, even though my grandfather remained a Pakistani citizen till his death (he missed the creation of Bangladesh by a year. I am sure he would have been extremely happy.).

There were others who have also shown such qualities. Jamshedji Tata[2] was born to Nusserwanji and Jeevanbai Tata on 3 March 1839 in Navsari, a small town in South Gujarat. Nusserwanji Tata was the first businessman in a family of Parsi Zoroastrian priests. He moved to Bombay and started trading. The rest is history.

There are others, big and small who have shown exemplary resilience in establishing enterprises here in India when we were under British rule. What sets some of them apart is the fact that these 'giants' could compete with British cotton fabrics and British steel in the market place and survive. There were no government subsidies. There were no easy finances. These were no concessional interests on funds. If at all any concessions

[2] Wikipedia

were given, they were given to British subjects.

Yet these 'giants' - I have named only two but there are many more - *survived* and built a Brand. They were men of vision and impeccable integrity.

After Independence, India became a changed place. This book is not about political history and I shall not dwell on it. However, it is a fact that India became utterly dependent on external aid and imports. In the late 1950s, we were gifted grain under the American statute P.L. 480. This remains a blot on the dignity of every Indian even today.

Did we ask ourselves how we could compete with our British rulers – who were leaders in industrial revolution – in steel, cotton fabrics and a host of products without technology support from the developed world? And more importantly, what changed after independence that we had to tour the developed world with a begging bowl? Even today, we cannot do without external aid.

Our status today is in many ways similar to the days of P.L. 480. Why do I say that? How is the past relevant to the present?

The entrepreneurship saga, at least that's what the buzz is today, started in the mid-1990s, revolving round the icon, Mr. Narayan Murthy. During the previous decades, the government, both in the states and at the center, tried to create similar ethos. Such government initiatives stemmed from unfulfilled promises of jobs made by political parties to millions of youth. The objective was to portray entrepreneurship as a viable career alternative. However, intent and implementation rarely match in a governmental ecosystem.

Others who were encouraged by Mr. Murthy are a class apart. Many have left jobs, or have decided against taking up a job. Either way they have a clear objective and are quite savvy about pitfalls. Some have networks that help them in developing their enterprise, of their own. This is quite in variance with what the government wanted to do.

Entrepreneurship is not a recent phenomenon. It has existed for a millennium and more. Certain disconnect and social apathy of a few decades has brought in this urgency, especially in the context of the globalized planet. My book shall try to hold forth some views, based on and backed by my experiences in the course of my 40 year saga as a first generation entrepreneur, case studies in mentoring individuals and groups in establishing enterprises during the past decade and a half, the sweet joy of success and the pangs of failure. I hope that my book could help bring hope to and inspire those who are at present fence sitters in delving into entrepreneurial ventures.

We must also understand that the 'Raja' – the King – is not the guy who has made his millions by amassing ill-gotten wealth, but the One who is in command of his livelihood. And to my mind that is the Entrepreneur.

CONTENTS

EXCERPT

Arindam Dutta : An Entrepreneurial Spirit

'A multi -dimensional personality, that Arindam Dutta is, has been my great pleasure to know and interact with for over a dozen years. With his background in Physics, and hands-on experience in production , marketing and management of some specialty products in his younger days, Arindam has passionately performed the complex role of nurturing and mentoring innovations and entrepreneurship among young academics of various disciplines in various institutions..........'

Prof (Dr) K. L. Chopra (Padamshri)
FNA, FASc, FNASc, FNAE, D.Sc.(hc)
(Former Director, Indian Institute of Technology, Kharagpur)

President , Society for Scientific Values

ACKNOWLEDGMENTS

My sincere thanks to my son Arijit and daughter Subhra, my wife Minakshi, dear friends, Dr. Chhaya Bhattacharya, Ms. Bratati Mukherji, entrepreneur Mr. Abhijit Sen, and surely, Prof K. Padmanabhan, University of Michigan at Dearborn. The one person who has been an anchor during my stints with various academic institutions has been Prof. K. L. Chopra. The critical inputs from them have been of immense value in finally completing this book.

1 WHY ENTREPRENEURSHIP

- It is a path towards fulfillment of a Dream.
- A path towards becoming an Achiever.
- An Entrepreneur must be emotionally prepared to continue on the path without being affected by the negatives at each turn.

Creating and Fulfilling Dreams

Manubhai Desai, the owner of India's most reputed home entertainment system manufacturer, Cosmic Stereo Systems, was my mentor.

I watched him working with the carpenters at the carpentry workshop of the factory, training them in skills in working with a new machine, or correcting a worker whose technique needed some tweaking.

I watched him open the bonnet of the vehicle when the car just refused to crank up. He would remain calm and collected. There were times, when visiting a friend over a drink in the evening, he would patiently listen to the host complaining about his music system's performance.

Manubhai would ask for a screwdriver, open up the equipment and take a look. Most often, all that was required to satisfy the host-customer was a minor adjustment. Such an attitude won the company a huge following.

I think the openness of a company to client feedback is the key to success. Customers will come back with suggestions or problems. Some customers do so because they want to be heard. However, some customers believe in a business's intent and capability to address their problem. This is a huge USP. *Never argue with your customer.* The customer is always right!

We built a bank of committed customers. Even if a friend would want to buy equipment overseas (which was sort of a status symbol of the rich and famous Mumbaikars those days), Manubhai would gladly guide him. He had half a dozen equipment guides that he would refer to, depending on the prospective buyer's budget.

Not only did it win him admiration, *Cosmic Stereo System was chosen as one of the gifts that Mrs. Indira Gandhi, the then Indian Prime Minister, carried with her to Bangladesh after the war for Sheikh Mujibur Rehaman, the legendary Bangladeshi freedom fighter and the first Prime Minister of Bangladesh. What an honour that was for Manubhai and his firm!*

Yes, he was proud of his achievements. We were all proud to be part of the team that brought the company to the forefront through its superior technology. A few of us were part of the technical team that carried out the final checks on the equipment meant for the Bangladesh P.M. We were justifiably elated!

Yet, Manubhai would hardly speak of such achievements (Cosmic won the Government of India Award for the 'nail less loudspeaker boxes' that he had designed). In those days, no one in India thought of patents.

My association with him from 1970 (it continues, though he has retired from active work) helped shape me as a person and, surely, as an entrepreneur.

There are many lessons to be learnt. It was one of 'sweepstakes wins' that brought me so close to this wonderful man. Even today, I wonder what I would have been doing otherwise. One thing is for certain, I would not have had the courage to launch a startup[3] in 1972.

Being an educated Bengali just out of his teens, and having studied in some of the most prestigious educational institutions in the country, brought with it a lot of baggage. It took me a while to unlearn the attitudes of the typical educated middle class[4]. At times I

---

[3] It was the worst of times. Bengal was agog with the Naxalite movement. Industries were fleeing the state in droves. The communists were on the warpath, holding *gheraos* (stopping work by demonstrating within office premises), demonstrations and bandhs (strikes that bring a city or area to a standstill). Jobs were scarce. Even today, looking back it feels scary.

wavered, when I would hear that a classmate has just joined a multi-national company, or successfully competed for a central government service job[5].

To me, sticking with the dream is the first challenge of an entrepreneur. Our planet earth is bombarded by millions of particles and cosmic rays every second. So is the human mind. The startup must work its way through all these forces towards a specific goal. Bengal, in those days, did not offer a favourable eco-system for startups. Only crooks succeeded in business – that was the accepted perception.

---

[4] It is not easy to unlearn. All of us who gained admissions to these premier institutions, actually a handful, had a *superior than thou* attitude, something similar to the present lot of IITians and those in IIMs. I am not talking of the newer lot that have gained admission to the expanded networks of these institutions in the past three years or so.

[5] The central government services of IFS (Foreign Service), IPS (Police Service), and IRS (Revenue Service) were the most coveted, along with the job of a probationary officer (PO) at the State Bank of India (SBI). If I remember right, the starting salary of a PO at SBI was higher than that of an IAS (Administrative Service) officer, whose first posting generally was in a remote district.

Concurrently, I joined Benares Hindu University for a graduate (MS) program in Physics under orders from my father. Once again, I wasn't sure whether my business will ever succeed. I was already toying with the idea of migrating to the US. How does a 21-year old guy, with no money, even think of defying the family? It was a diktat! Alternately, my thoughts ranged towards enrolling for a PhD. One evening, when I returned to my hostel, the warden, Prof. Mukherjee[6] was speaking to a few students, whom he introduced as his research scholars. These scholars were discussing their immediate need for a job. Since the university had no vacancy, they had planned to appear for a clerkship examination at a reputed bank.

I was quite shocked! I stayed up that night trying to make sense of what made Physics researchers even consider a position of a clerk in a bank!

Years later, I came to realize that whatever may be our area of study, we should have the capacity to add value to one's individual self. Education must help us adapt in varying situations. There is no point dreaming of becoming another Albert Einstein. What is the point? How many such Einsteins have emerged in the past 100 years?

---

[6] Prof Mukherji had completed his dissertation in the US and was a tenured professor of nuclear physics in our department.

Entrepreneurs are Leaders

There are quite a few entrepreneurs who are leaders in their fields. Let me name two – Mr. Narayan Murthy and Dr. (Ms.) Kiran Majumder Shaw.

Mr. Murthy ventured into IT at a time when India was debating the basic efficiency of the computer. A vocal section of the people (led by militant trade union leaders) felt that it was a tool to replace people in the workplace. There was reference to the classic 'Modern Times' by Charlie Chaplin. The government stood on the side-line. How Mr. Murthy succeeded is a story that has been narrated a million times. He and his company are icons. Dr. Ms. Majumder is a qualified Brew Master who diversified in bio-technology, when it was not even in the curriculum of any teaching institution here in India. She started from a garage, and today Bio-Con leads the way in bio-technology in India.

In 1980, one of the companies I was associated with decided to assemble desktop photo copiers. Till then very few companies used a photo copying machine in-house .

We started negotiating with a couple of Japanese manufacturers, both of whom were, and still are, very large corporations. By 1982, we did bring in fully assembled machines for test marketing. Unfortunately, all the machines malfunctioned. India is a country with temperate climate and high humidity.

All its metros, except Delhi, have a very high level of humidity. Delhi sizzles in summer. Air-conditioners were expensive.

We then started negotiating with Canon. Since Canon had already collaborated with one corporate house, they could not offer us their robust Desktop Copier NP270/271. Instead, they offered their PC series, which was capable of A4 size copies only. Moreover, the load handling capacity of the PC series was much lower than that of the NP series.

NP series was priced at Rs.1.75 lacs and the PC series at Rs.50 thousand. These are 1983 prices. Today, one can buy a computer/printer copier (A4) for office and personal use for Rs. 6 thousand. Given these numbers, it becomes easy to see why very few business houses had copiers at that time.

The NP series used an older technology. However, these were heavy duty printers. Before we could approach the market with the PC series copiers, we had to establish support services in all major metros. It took us all of five months to execute the first sale of the PC series.

Copiers, subsequently, became the mainstay of any business. Today no business can do without a printer copier.

Technology driven startups do chart a new path. Apple's iPhone is an example. There are others too.

Certain assumptions need to be made. First and foremost, startups do not have deep pockets. The technical team is almost completely involved in the technical brilliance of their invention. The problem is they are by then wallowing in their own glory. As a mentor, time and again I have found it difficult to pull them out of that particular orbit.

Secondly, they need to be focused on the end use and the end user of that technology. In 1974, Cosmic Music System launched a high powered, high fidelity amplifier and named it LAB3000. It took music lovers by storm. The cost of the system – amplifier, loudspeaker, turntable and stereo tape deck - would create a crater in any person's pocket. Yet, we got a sizable number of customers.

We, from the tech team, wanted the amplifier to be feature-rich. We wanted to prove our technical superiority. Some of our customers would buy the amplifier (only the unit), take it abroad, and match it with loudspeakers and other accessories.

One facility we did build in was Karaoke, which as a system came into India in the late 1980s and early 1990s. But our beta customers found the switching system very complicated. Ultimately, we decided not to implement it. One must keep in mind that electronic components that are commonplace today were not available then. All our critical components had to be imported. The circuit design, the printed circuit board, the electrical wiring, the chassis, the cabinet and a few other components were manufactured locally. Our inputs were limited to the design of the critical electronic circuits. Some of our competitors copied circuits of leading names. But these copied circuits never gave the desired output.

But what happened to such companies that had played a critical leadership role in India way back in the 1970s and 1980s? Unfortunately, all of them, or nearly all, folded up after the government suddenly announced the liberal industrial policy in 1991-92.

I would like to offer my set of reasons:

Lack of professional management: Nearly all these companies were controlled by members of a single family. Leaders lacked clarity in their vision under the parameters set by government policy.

Inability to predict the wide ranging changes to the socialistic government policy by 1992: The policy was further relaxed in subsequent years. Overseas companies were given free access to the Indian market. It was a tsunami that hit the industry, big and small, without warning.

2 BUSINESS

- The Entrepreneurship Journey is lonely. In socialist countries, like India, it is not the primary focus of civil society, the government and the political eco-system.
- In the past 2 decades and more, entrepreneurs, whose names are common parlance today, have all gone through pretty rough times. Many others have perished and therefore, we do not know who they were.
- An entrepreneur needs a Mentor. A Mentor is like a Guru in the Guru-Sishya-Parampara.

Indian business had very little exposure to global business. Even the export houses that did some global business, concentrated on Africa, the Middle East and a few Southeast Asian countries in exporting food grains and some engineering goods of questionable quality.

Brand consciousness of the Indian customer: As global brands flooded the market, the demand for local brands all but dried up. Needless to say, some of the global brands later withdrew from the market for various logistic reasons. Today, the Indian market offers a wide choice of global brands in televisions, mobile phones, computers, edible products, apparels and other products (an entire range of global products are available in nearly every sphere of activity. In effect, India today is part of the global market). I am happy to note a few local companies do exist and make their presence felt.

As I have mentioned, the earlier Indian companies were family controlled, did not have professionals who could explore the possibilities of technology and market tie ups with global players. In one of the companies I was involved with the company that manufactured the Canon photo-copying machine (later resigned in 1986). The Managing Director had poor communication skills (he was comfortable communicating in Hindi). I wish he had considered using an interpreter as the situation changed. The Japanese and the Chinese do it even today.

It was not just about creating a relationship. Foreign companies ask for a host of data from Indian counterparts, including market projections that have to include extensive market research data.

None of companies I had been involved with ever paid attention to these aspects. The government had announced the new policy in 1991, literally, overnight (the treasury of the central government had run out of funds and was on the point of sovereign default in debt repayments). However, one cannot reinvent work ethic overnight. Nor can one collect meaningful data so quickly.

The silver lining I see today is a long list of successful Indian startups. At the same time, I salute those that perished at the critical point. Surely their initiatives must also be lauded. The market place is in a state of perpetual motion. When we speak of the market and marketing, we must realize that *market* cannot be simply defined as the place or process of buying and selling. Making money is the final goal in any business. But the entire process of being paid is way too complex.

The eco-system in our colleges is one that mollycoddles the student. I am not speaking of the microscopic minority that comes from deprived community[7]. Despite all talk of support to these backward communities, it would take years before youngsters from these communities make the grade. Gaining admission to a college requires a graded approach: clearing class ten exams, then the class twelve exams. Only then a college education could become a reality. Getting admission to a University like BHU requires

[7] During my PG program at BHU, a few of my classmates were from villages that, till the early 70s, did not have electricity and no motorable road. The nearest bus stop was some 2-5 miles away. They never complained about food, the heat or the quality of hostel accommodation. I found them focused on their studies. I don't recall their discussing movies that were on in theaters in Varanasi.

a pretty high level of academic achievement.

Why do I say 'could'? I have employed a young woman who has completed school till class ten. I asked her why she stopped her education there. She said that the family decided to spend the money on her brother's education. And this is an incident in Kolkata, where access to an educational institution in terms of logistics and numbers is rather easy. I can only imagine the issues involved in rural areas and smaller towns.

But most students that enroll, come from well off middle class or wealthy families. The family is the provider for the entire four-year period (for a technology program; others are three-year programs) in college. This includes tuition fees, boarding and lodging, travel thrice a year at least, during academic recess, cost of study materials, entertainment allowance and of course the cost towards maintaining a mobile handset.

From time to time, the student places various demands on the family – a new computer, clothes, short holidays with college friends etc. Though I have mentioned well off middle class families, yet at times they too are financially stretched. But the Indian family would never utter a word of protest, more so if the student is a boy. Many families dip into their savings[8] to provide for such expenses.

And this is not the end of the road. After

[8] I personally know of instances where the family mortgaged their house to provide funds.

graduating, many students want to enroll for a MBA program. This entails an expensive coaching program (these train students to clear the CAT or Common Entrance Test or similar entrance exams) to begin with. The cheapest MBA degree program would cost not less than Rs. 7 lacs[9]. I remember asking a potential candidate who came from a business family, as to why the amount could not be invested in a business in which his family is already involved. With the plethora of B-schools, with extremely poor quality of faculty, that dot the country, the quality of graduates can only be poor. And naturally, jobs are scarce. The associations of business and industries have officially told the government that quality of technology and management graduates are such that most of them are un-employable.

Six years after the student has completed Class twelve, he is ready to be employed. But who can guarantee that this student will start earning the day he steps out of the college portal?

Most technical institutions tom tom placements, which really means a job in a BPO (Business Process Outsourcing Company) with an entry level salary around Rs.15 thousand[10] a month. Further, the

[9] As I put this figure on paper, I realize that it will rise many fold before the book is printed.

[10] These are compensation packages offered by

centers of such employment are Mumbai, Delhi / Gurgaon/ Noida, Pune, Hyderabad, Bangalore and Chennai. Those who are not residents of these metros, have to relocate. The family, yet again, finances the cost of relocation.

Students who wish to become entrepreneurs[11] are, generally, a pampered lot. Many amongst them have a fairy tale image of the 'Entrepreneur'. They get carried away with the fame and money associated with names such as Mr. Murthy, Steve Jobs and Bill Gates. I wish they took the trouble to study the backgrounds of these very successful men, the period preceding their success. How Steve jobs spent his years after high school sleeping on the dorm floor, of going without meals. Or how Sudha Murthy (Mr. Murthy's wife) struggled to fund the family and also the enterprise of Mr. Murthy and his team members[12].

'Baptism by Fire' is a phrase that keeps ~~appearing time and again in my writings. One~~

large companies. I am told the figure could be as low as Rs. 5 thousand. Unfortunately, I do not have any means available to verify this.

[11] Leading B-Schools publish compensation packages at the top end of the scale. Of late, some schools have begun publishing average compensation numbers. Unfortunately, we never come to know of the lowest accepted package.

[12] All this is available in the public domain.

need not develop an iPhone for a livelihood. A samosa[13] shop in a moderate sized town probably would do. I think it would do eminently well. All that one needs are, potato, flour, *kadhai (wok or frying pan)*, stove and cooking oil.

But I think that what keeps troubling the youth is that an engineering degree coupled with an MBA just does not gel. It does not guarantee success as an entrepreneur. Real Estate development is big business in India today, especially in housing projects. In reality, some, if not most, 'realty' operations are borderline illegal. Yet, some engineers and MBAs have ventured into 'realty'. The aim is to provide quality and affordable housing. Though it sounds good on paper, quality and affordable housing is a myth in India. A realtor can, without know-how or effort, either copy designs from the web or from existing structures. All he needs to do next is to catch hold of an unemployed architect and translate the design on paper, and voila, he's done. Rest is easy. Hardly any investments are required. Do a little research and you would know why.

I am not deriding 'realtors' or the realty business. I believe that it is the quickest route to becoming a millionaire. Sure, there could be quite a few run-ins with the law. Well, 'you win some, lose some'.

---

[13] A savory snack popular in India

But this book is not about *get rich quick*. I am also not going to debate the pros and cons. I am sold on the idea, that a youngster using his intellectual prowess and an uncommon appetite for risk can make it big.

Just as Mr. Murthy (I keep coming back to him), a successful entrepreneur is the 'light house' for the talented youth of the country. Some of the enterprises that have become immensely successful in recent times in India are *'makemytrip.com'*, *'flipkart.com'* and a few others. Some software developer teams have also created successful apps for tablets, mobile phones etc. It is these types of enterprises today that drive the youth in their entrepreneurial quest. It also helps if the brand gets it due prominence in the business arena.

3 ENTREPRENEURSHIP

- What is the role of the government in driving entrepreneurship?
- The IT and ITeS business started in the 1980s, when the government and political parties had vociferously objected to the use of computers. It had led to demonstrations and violence on the streets. Today, the IT sector is the largest employer of white collar workers.
- The IT initiative is led by startups.

Government's Role in Entrepreneurship

Most state governments in the country talk of attracting investments for the state. In reality, the governments want large capital inflows. On the face of it, large investments also help the state earn large taxes. But, it is equally true that politicians do not play with a straight bat. We see various shady deals being carried out. Today, the media is proactive and people, at large, keep a track of the goings on. Even if we ignore such dealings (surely some dealings are 'clean'), over the years the condition of the downtrodden do not seem to have improved. Government figures say over 30% of the urban population[14] are below the poverty line.

State governments also talk of inclusive growth. Such talks are a must, as all political parties realize, that without a pep talk on the improvement of the plight of the poor they would find it difficult to succeed at the hustings.

It is a proven fact that SMEs contribute 40% to the GDP of the country and are the largest employers. The statistics of the government is incomplete as a large number of SMEs do not register.

What stops SMEs from following government rules? Harassment at government offices! I remember a few months after the EDC (Entrepreneurship Development Cell) started operations in Kolkata, a startup team of qualified media personnel approached me for advice. During the discussion, one team member asked me why their application for a municipal trade license had been pending for eight months. I was aware of this issue. The inspectors were excepting a hefty bribe. How do I tell a team of youngsters with a dream, that they ought to pay the speed money? I, who am representing a reputed teaching institution of the country and the city, baulked at the very idea. Honestly, for the first time I felt

[14] World Bank 25/2/11

disgusted at my inability in finding a solution to a seemingly simple issue.

On visiting any metro city of the country, one will find thousands of venders selling wares on the streets – items covering the entire gamut of products and, of course, food. And officially, a food stall requires a police license, a health license and a host of others that add up to a minimum of some dozen approvals.

These people just don't care. Instead they pay off the local police and their minders. Such payments are well structured (usually weekly) and nobody defaults. Any non-payment will lead to suspension of their business.

The situation raises some critical questions. Why is the government not trying to bring such entrepreneurs into the main stream? When these guys are ready to pay, why don't the authorities collect the taxes? We cannot expect all these street vendors to fill up government application forms. They do not understand the process; most of them are 'semi-literate'. I agree that some conditions must be adhered to. But there must be differentiation between a one-person enterprise and the likes of the Taj and Marriots.

If the government has initiated the Anganwadi Volunteer Scheme in rural areas, why can it not be extended to the urban populace? It is well known that huge disparities between opportunities and incomes between rural and urban areas have led to unchecked migration to our cities. Check the railway bookings from Mumbai during festive seasons, when these people try to make their annual visit to their native villages. As an example, the artisans in the jewelry trade in Mumbai are largely from Murshidabad in West Bengal. Now some illegal migrants from Bangladesh also find their way in, as Murshidabad lies close to the Indo-Bangladesh border.

Why can't we create a hub for these artisans in Murshidabad, like Gujarat did decades back in Surat for the Diamond trade? Indians have an inherent streak of entrepreneurship. Yes, most of them are small. Therefore, we, the civil society, and the law makers ought to strive in finding ways and means for facilitating their growth to a medium size enterprise.

During the Q & A session at a seminar, a participant asked this question in reference to the pathetic state of West Bengal's economy. A valid question in my opinion. Not only would such organic growth create more employment, it would contribute to the state's coffers.

Entrepreneurs are the major employers in any country. Being startups, they do not hesitate in employing unskilled persons, who are subsequently trained on the job. At my health center I initially employed graduates to man my reception. The work – the front office – is repetitive in nature. After some time, the employee would find another job and leave. A front-office job at my health center is hardly commensurate with the skills of a graduate.

I was in a quandary. We also had female attendants at the clinic. I experimented with the attendant manning the reception desk, along with my regular receptionist. This approach has worked well. Today, I, at any one point of time, have two receptionist-cum-attendants. They are quite happy with their job profile. None of them are graduates. They have just completed class ten. And, as a bonus, one of them lives in the same locality where my clinic is located. Not only has it helped the clinic earn the goodwill of the people in the area, I too have a feel-good factor for being able to provide a better quality job to people who, otherwise, would have been working either as a domestic help, or a roving sales person selling cheap and poor quality consumer goods.

Once this approach worked in one of my health care centers, we immediately duplicated it in the other one. In both the centers we found the staff, so selected, eminently teachable, and also very diligent in their duties. Rain or sunshine, you will hardly ever see them missing.

There is another issue involved with the infusion of large capital, be it in industry or healthcare. Today, states compete with one another to attract investors. The small investors, I feel, are largely ignored.

Let us take the case of healthcare. All governments today give subsidies in the purchase of land for establishing a hospital. Some states have a rider that such facilities will be eligible provided they are outside the municipal limits of the city[15]. In Kolkata, such hospitals have been established just outside the legal boundaries of the municipality. It surely negates the spirit of the policy.

Further, requirements are polyclinics in rural areas across the state. The argument is that no serious medical practitioner would be willing to visit those. This is an erroneous statement. The polyclinics in rural and *mofussil* towns have poor infrastructure. Doctors would surely visit provided the facilities are the same as that I have at my clinic – clean spreads on the examination table, clean rest rooms, a telephone to speak to the doctor and a receptionist to attend to patient queries. Nothing extraordinary!

A person suffering from any malady first needs a doctor to diagnose. We find from our experience at our clinic over the past 23 years, 90% of the patients recover through simple medication. It is the remaining 10% that need further advanced treatment.

[15] These hospitals under the rules are supposed to set aside a percentage of beds for poor nonpaying patients. Few do so.

It is the lack of healthcare facilities that force people in rural areas to come to the city. A reputed city hospital is the only place where they feel safe and where they are sure to find the doctor who would provide the necessary treatment.

But all this costs a packet. Besides, travelling to the city, the cost of board and lodging of the patient and the person accompanying him/her is high. And I am not computing the loss of wages for the number of days the person is staying in the city.

The fanfare of government policies towards encouraging establishment of hospitals is so high, that entrepreneurs who could contribute in establishing a good polyclinic get the feeling that a polyclinic business will never work as there is no *'demand'* for such services. A terrible fallacy this is.

From the '50s, India has planned its economy through the five-year plans. The planners have all along come up with various forecast. We have been regaled with the brilliance of the economists and other experts who are involved in such planning. I have seen the food riots of 1964 in Kolkata, 17 years after India gained independence. The present government (2009 onwards) had predicted the growth of GDP at more than 8%. For the past year, an enormous increase of the prices of food across the board has caused great concern. But the planners always have some excuses. Recently the government agreed that the growth will not touch 8% of GDP (now the official estimate is less than 5% for FY 2012-13) for reasons that now the planners have come up with.

This reminds me about the forecast by astrologers. Anyone who visits an astrologer is first told about his past. Most people who visit astrologers are amazed by the near perfect past history. When the astrologer speaks of the future, the client is mesmerized. I have tried to understand the pattern. I found that the astrologer speaks of the future in terms that would be interpreted in ways *more than one*. The clients interpret it in their own fashion. Our planners are no better. It is time to involve the huge population of the country in a productive initiative. The government ought to identify the areas where people are interested in growing their business and/or helping them with alternate opportunity to invest in.

Technology is a critical enabler. Unfortunately, till date, we do not have any means – including sophisticated software – that can predict a sure shot application that would keep our cash machines whirring. I only wish such software does evolve in future.

Today, all we can do after studying various parameters predict the optimum path. This is nothing new. Tools for such prediction have been in use for quite a few decades with varying degrees of success and of course failures. The current tools in use have a higher degree of sophistication.

The government, however, has the wherewithal in identifying areas that need certain services. I wish these areas are notified through a website along with what the government believes are the facilities that need to be established. The present government of Mamata Banerjee in West Bengal is trying to follow this path[16]. The clarity of such notifications is a must. We have seen instances where the government has announced that so many thousands of teachers would be employed in primary schools. The education departments too had notified the intended appointments. But the actual recruitment and postings in schools have taken years. The aspirants surely lose hope in the interim period and quite a few competent teachers are forced to take up other jobs or leave the state in quest of one.

Paradoxically, a small section of the business community flourished during the same period. No it was not their cutting edge technology. It was more to do with their excellent acumen in 'wheeling dealing'. They were neither manufacturers nor traders. Yes, they had companies that claimed to be one or both of these. Actually the signboard was the only indication of the company. After a few months the board too disappeared. Such people still operate the markets. It is only in the past couple of years that their expertise

[16] Early days, we need to wait for the results to show.

has made media headlines and some, I think a microscopic few, are cooling their heels in prison. India tightened it fiscal laws after mid-2000, that too in stages.

I think that small-timers like us who could hang on till today have excellent management skills and of course the blessings of 'lady luck'. Why do I say management skills? A number of small-timers tried to follow the wheeler dealers in obtaining loans from bank. And then they sat pretty assuming that over the years the bank would write-off bad loans. May be some banks did. Now I see that the banks have cracked their whip on such defaulters. What makes me sad is that money owed by most of these people is so little? I fail to understand as to why they did not keep a line of communication open with their bankers[17]. Instead the matter now is before the DRT[18].

Seldom, I hear of major defaulters being brought to book. A few years back the IT major Satyam Computers admitted to fraud amounting to Rs.15,000 crores ($3b approx.). Yet, the company accounts were being audited and accepted by their banks, the

[17] Some of their friends had wrongly advised to keep quiet and the matter will go away on its own. It was not all foolish advice as in the 70s and early 80s such write off by bankers ware not very uncommon. Those days the banks would file a civil suit, if at all, and those would take years.

[18] Debt Recovery Tribunal

auditors and the regulators of the government. I am yet to fathom as to how this was being done, when each set of regulators were different sets of people and the fraud was run for a period of nearly six years. Amazing!

This is just one case that has come to light. Over the past 64 years there have been quite a few but as we are all aware, after a while the matter just disappears. Why am I raking these up now?

As I have mentioned earlier on, the 'wheeler dealers' are very much alive and kicking. Startups that venture in the market are bound to meet them and might get influenced. The guys are influential and know the right people and get the right connections. But, one must keep in mind that the present eco-system in the country is quite at variance with what it was earlier. There were no Right to Information laws, no Central Vigilance Commission and to top it all no Anna Hazare movement. Today, the ever powerful political class is cautious.

Looking Beyond

Today we have access to the entire globe through the net, literally from a remote corner of country, where 15 years back a working telephone would be a prized possession. There is no need to approach these 'wheeler dealers' to get a contract. We can fix the price of our services and/or product on absolute business terms – one on one. There is no question of kickbacks. I strongly recommend keeping a distance from these 'wheeler dealers', who today operate under the guise of a fancy consultant, usually based in the capital city of Delhi[19]. I am sure the recent telecom 2G case that has caught the attention of the nation has brought forth attention to such consultants. But there are hundreds out there.

Startups must be ready to face the turmoil of such a socio-political system. One cannot build an enterprise hoping to be in a cocoon[20]. Let us all take heart from the vast multitude of small traders and small family-driven enterprises that dot our country. Many of the owners have no formal education; some who do, have no clue as to 'how to work the system'. They are not slick. They cannot afford to be. Yet they are able to provide for their families basic necessities of life. I am sure they would love to better their lot with better housing, clothes *et al.* But the goal looks elusive. Yet they are stoical. Let us also

---

[19] The capital city is known for its opulent houses in plush suburbs with a fleet of fancy cars. One would be hard to find as to what is the occupation of the owners. These are the high powered brokers that deal from pin to ministerial berths in the cabinet. The recent 2G scam has brought forth some of the sordid deals out in public gaze.

[20] As Bill Gates has noted-there is nothing fair in life.

learn from them.

Some of what I have written may sound very negative from the point of view of venturing in a Greenfield enterprise. I must admit that most of the successful startups I have mentored have taken all hurdles in their stride. In some cases we have had multiple discussions on how to overcome such hurdles. A supportive family is a great help. The dream of the entrepreneur in achieving the goal drowns the negatives that he could be facing. Thomas Friedman in his book, 'From Beirut to Jerusalem' speaks of the resilience of people in the strife-torn Beirut over a period of 14 years. He goes on to say that the residents have found their salvation through unique mind games.

I believe all of us small-time entrepreneurs must be subconsciously playing such mind games in trying to forge ahead.

Just the other day an entrepreneur approached me with a proposal in marketing 'ice candy'. He had already carried out a short market survey. He was sounding very upbeat. I then started asking him about the various clearances he requires from government agencies in marketing the product. At first he was pretty cool. As we progressed with the discussion, I realized that he was getting nervous. Actually he did not know of these. And now he had no clue as to how to go about. Welcome to the world of enterprise.

Innovation has been the key to human civilization over the centuries[21]. The last decade of the 20th century has seen a phenomenal rise in the knowledge[22] led Innovative initiatives. What is noteworthy that the new impetus comes nearly a century after the Industrial revolution has created a remarkable economic growth.

While the Industrial revolution[23] created a new economic order in the European continent and the US, it left out large parts of this planet. Of course Japan was a unique exception.

---

[21] Horses have been used in warfare 5000 years ago. There are evidence of chariots been used by 1600BC in the near East.-Wikipedia

[22] The present day Innovations have largely emanated from teaching institutions. I call this knowledge led to distinguish with the previous ones in a sense, though those too were the outcome of the human mind.

[23]In the two centuries following 1800, the world's average per capita income increased over 10-fold, while the world's population increased over 6-fold.[2] In the words of Nobel Prize winner Robert E. Lucas, Jr., "For the first time in history, the living standards of the masses of ordinary people have begun to undergo sustained growth. ... Nothing remotely like this economic behavior has happened before."[3]-Wikipedia

1960-90 saw the rise of the ASEAN Tigers[24]. Small countries like Korea and Taiwan could establish large capital intensive corporations that are leaders in the world in their respective fields even today.

The world is riding a new economic order with the BRIC nations showing very promising economic growth.

---

[24] Is a term used in reference to the highly developed economies of Hong Kong, Singapore, South Korea and Taiwan after 1970. These regions were the first newly-industrialized regions, noted for maintaining exceptionally high growth rates and rapid industrialization between the early 1960s and 1990s. By the 21st century, all four regions have since graduated into advanced economies and high-income economies.

4 INDIAN SAGA

- Except in specific cities, and the state of Gujarat, entrepreneurship is actually a non-starter, if one realizes the size of the India population.
- Instead, there is a powerful brokers' lobby across the country. This lobby is active in wheeling-dealing. Mind blogging sums change hands. This, I am sure, is not the form of entrepreneurship we, in India, should be looking at.

India, from where I come, has shown remarkable resilience[25] and for the past decade and more has clocked compounded rate of growth.

It is no secret that the catalyst for this growth has been Information Technology. India has top class software professionals and Indian companies are global players in IT. For the past decade India has seen the growth in Biotechnology. It is today one of the major manufacturers of generic formulations in

[25] In spite of the 2008 economic meltdown that crippled economies in many countries across the world.

pharma[26].

Such an economic windfall in India brought forth enhanced employment opportunities to the educated youth. The educated class in India always looked for white collared jobs. Pre-1990, it was the few government jobs that were most sought. Obviously such an avenue could benefit just a handful. Unfortunately, these jobs created a new class[27]

[26] Many Indian drug manufacturers have been able to enter the US markets. An example is the foundation's drug research strategy revolved around searching for analogues but its changed focus to innovative R&D, hiring new scientists – especially Indian students studying abroad on doctoral and post-doctoral courses. In 2000, foundation set up a US lab in Atlanta, dedicated to discovery and design of novel therapeutics. The lab is called Reddy US Therapeutics Inc. (RUSTI) and its main aim is the discovery of next-generation drugs using genomics and proteomics. Reddy's research thrust focused on large niche areas in western markets – anti-cancer, anti-diabetes, cardiovascular and anti-infection drugs.

[27]Whereby the status of government employees in the marriage market was very high, with multiple marriage offers with lucrative financial benefits from the brides' families.

in our society. It did create social tensions too.

The Information Technology brought forth jobs at extremely lucrative salary structures. The youth found an avenue for better prospects that relied more on competence and deliveries rather than years of experience and bountiful grey hairs. This new found economic wealth spawned other service sectors[28] such as hospitality, transport, shopping malls and advanced health care systems. A section of the populace did not have to rely on archaic government health services, nor did they have to use 'influence' with some bureaucrat for use of such facilities.

This brought to the fore in India a new domain - The Knowledge Enterprise. In the past 3 decades IT has brought in the limelight people as Mr. Narayan Murthy, Mr. Azim Premji and others from the IT domain. Today I believe the youth is far more enthused by a man as Mr. Murthy[29] than by any other in the country. His story –Infosys –

---

[28] Indian have successfully established and grown companies in various sectors in the past decade and a half that are household names today.

[29] People have been influenced by his grit, honesty and surely the phenomenal Success. Of the three characteristic Mr. Murthy comes forth as a person of innate simplicity and clean image.

is a bible that every school and college going kid is aware. His success story of rags to riches has enthused qualified youth to venture as entrepreneurs. No initiative of the government has and will ever work, unless the society can identify with a person in flesh and blood. This is what Murthy has contributed to the Entrepreneurship initiative as a 'Career Alternate' for the large numbers of educated youth[30] of the country.

Incubators, the contemporary concept in ~~driving knowledge startups in~~ India are

[30] 2.2m people are expected to migrate from developing countries to the developed one till the year 2050 - http://www.thegff.com/Groups/175830/Global_Futures_and/Reports/The_Future_report/The_Future_report.aspx

[31] There are a few privately held and administered incubators too. A good beginning.

[32]In case of an incubator down in South India that was gamely trying to sustain a company re-conditioning crankshaft/axle for diesel locomotives. Of course the scale of production was very low and these companies had no projections to power growth and diversify. The others were no better.

largely funded by the federal government[31]. As per the current policy of the government these must be academic incubators, though in a few cases some exceptions have been made. Therefore all these incubators are located within academic or R&D institutions. The government has taken some steps to see that the incubators function independently.

As recent as 1998, hardly 4 or 5 incubators were functioning in the entire country. Most of these were struggling to induct startups. Though IT in the commercial domain had taken off very successfully, most of these Incubators were saddled with small workshops manufacturing small tools and implements[32].

Today Entrepreneurship is a buzzword. Nearly all technical institutions have an entrepreneurship cell[33]. In most cases these are ably managed by the students. There have been few success stories. Some of the pass outs of such institutions have kept in touch and act as mentors[34] to the cell. There are inter-institutional Business Plan competitions[35]. Students have become familiar with the

[33] These cells are into Student activities more like a club.

[34] I shall deal with the subject of Mentor later in my submission.

[35] Usually it is an annual event. The students make an effort to get sponsors from Industry. These sponsorships are very small amounts, barely covers their cost.

concept of VCs and Angel fund managers. They understand to some extent the funding pattern needed and what it means when a group exits a company. Yes, this decade has ramped up the awareness in entrepreneurship across the country, at least within some of the college going community.

India has culturally been an entrepreneurial community. As Shakespeare would say we have been a nation of shop keepers and petty traders. However at the beginning of the 20th century Indian entrepreneurs set up major industries particularly in steel and cotton cloth. There were some very enterprising persons who also set up companies in pharma and chemicals. It was indeed a very heartening initiative as India under British rule till 1947, had to import everything from Britain or from British colonies. Steel and cotton was the mainstay of the British economy and it thrived through exports at prices controlled by our rulers.

After independence India adapted the Russian system of development and the state became the driver of the economy[36], building major power plants, steel mills. The government nationalized major industries in natural resources, banks and Insurance.

Private enterprises were strictly controlled

[36] Incorporated the famous 5 Year Plan and an equally huge department called the Planning Commission.

through an elaborate system of licenses and checks initiated by a retinue of government inspectors. It gave rise to systemic corruption. Even after two decades of 'liberalization'[37] we find the cancerous growth having affected the top echelons of government.

A very specific section of the business community did flourish. This group is still very active, as money does speak. I remember that after the new policy was announced by the government dismantling the 'license raj' (1991-92), a correspondent wrote a column in the Economic Times[38] where he was very candid in admitting that business in India was the skill in manipulating and selling industrial licenses.

The spirit of entrepreneurs was decimated post-independence. Today what we see is a new generation that has been spared the ignominy of the 'license raj[39]'. The

[37] A change of government policies on Industrial licensing, overseas tie-ups and easing of remittances overseas, in the past decade and half India has seen a phenomenal growth of tourist traffic both inward and outward. The government direct and indirect tax collections have risen to levels that earlier economists could not ever imagine.

[38] The correspondent, if I remember right was a gentleman named Jhunjhunwala who was a mill owner in Rajasthan. Economic Times is a leading financial daily.

government woke up to the fact that Entrepreneurship ought to be a Career Option as it was in no position to provide employment to the vast numbers of youth under 35 years[40].

Asia Pacific comprises of countries having diverse *political, religious, geographical and cultural* background. Only one country has shown a unique resolve in climbing the economic ladder, despite a war and the atomic bombs.

Today the mood in the country is quite in variance to what it was in the 70s, 80s and even in the 90s. At least a fairly large section of the civil society has turned vocal. And it is heartening to watch the younger apolitical group leading the protests. I wish such actions by the civil society remains unabated. Without the civil society as watchdog, I shudder to think what could happen to the future of the country and the youngsters who today are in school or right there as first time voters in elections for the assembly and the parliament.

There are enough avenues for the business to strive within the parameters of the law. Having said that, it should also be our goal to

[39] The Licensing system and the inspectors were labeled as 'license raj' and 'inspector raj' respectively.

[40] India has 70% of its population under the age of 35.

ask for change of such laws, that are either archaic or mala-fide. Yes, it is a tough call. But as the going gets tough we must all get tougher[41]. What worries me that such rampant rise in corrupt practices, in days to come, may tempt business and administration to adopt unfair means to earn the quick buck to the detriment of the people of the country. I am sure all of us do not want a repeat of Satyam Computer episode. I am distressed by the pain felt by the employees of the company who labored to create a huge institution that in a day just faded after the scam broke. A pity!!

Today, there are quite a few midsized IT companies run by educated Indians that are engaged with business activities in the global scale. Let these people have the chance to prosper and place India on the global map like Korea, Taiwan have done decades earlier.

Earning money in business is very important. But we see quite a few businesses of 'money making'. As an example 'Chit Fund' (Ponzi scheme) is a business that works in collecting funds from ordinary folks. For the past few

---

[41] The Singur and Nandigram movement claimed many lives and lot many people were injured, property was burned down, looted women were molested. Bengal at that point was under communist rule where the communists always took decisions in the name of the common people. It proves that once in power their definition of the common people undergoes radical changes.

decades we hear of the government making some noises about regulating them. Yet, these businesses flourish. It's worrying. It is just like any 'Ponzi' scheme. Bernard Madoff has been sentenced to 100 years plus in prison. I don't remember any in India has yet been imprisoned. India has an excellent judicial infrastructure. Justice must be seen to be done. This is what our department of justice must ensure.

Our knowledge driven startups comprises of talented people. I am mentoring a few of them for the past few years. I know what I am talking about. Nurturing a startup culture in the country will help create wealth for the nation. And let us not forget these enterprises are tomorrow's employers. This too is very important as the government has constantly lagged behind in their promises of providing gainful employment to the vast numbers that are still un-employed. It is time all including the political parties realize that we as a country do not have the financial clout to employ all these people. In the past 64 years the governments have skirted the issue of providing a social net. The government has admitted that funds meant for the weaker sections do not reach them. There is large scale leakage of funds. Plus the cost of administration of such funds keep rising owing to frequent wage revisions of government employees, while the poor unemployed just pray and hope.

5 THE CIVIL SOCIETY

- The entrepreneurship roadmap crisscrosses various government regulations and statutory norms. Starting any venture is not a single-window clearance.
- Talk to entrepreneurs who are already in the business. It always helps to be fore warned.

Indians do have some very positive traits that are a boon for a country as India with diverse culture and languages. The first that comes to mind is our affinity to the family. This includes the extended family. Even in the 21st century it is very common to find people staying in joint families – grandfather, grandmother, siblings and their families and so on. I have lived in a joint family for years during my school days. Some uncle or aunt would be ready to help me out with my school work. It was really fun. There would be some celebrations every month –puja, birthdays, just a get together, games. I never missed the fact that I hardly had an opportunity for an outing planned just for me as in any nuclear family. It was fun time.

We do not hesitate to participate in religious festivals whether it is Christmas, Easter, Id or Durga Puja. We would at times visit a church, Gurudwara[42] and a temple with the same reverence. There was always the sense of instant camaraderie. One sees this everywhere. At any tourist spot you will find people chatting with absolute strangers. Yes, as people, we are inclusive.

Having said all this, there are some very strong negative characteristics. The first that come to my mind is the definite lack of hygiene. No, I would not like to give examples, except it is nothing to do with the economic well-being of the person/persons unless the person has been incapacitated by extreme poverty and hunger (this is also a scenario that is very true). We would like to have an 'intimate' chat that normally would be audible to nearly everybody in the room. We believe in jostling. Go to any function, funeral, marriage or a simple queue for the local transport, you are sure to be jostled.

We also believe in fawning. At any function if a celebrity turns up, the majority of the invitee would be making a bee line for the celebrity, leaving the host of the function high and dry.

---

[42]The place of worship for the Sikh community.

After the Satyam scam broke, what came to the fore was definite penchant by a section of the new generation entrepreneurs in get rich quick mode.

Frankly I have not researched any of the scams that have come to light in the recent past. I find the news pretty disheartening. Whatever I write here on the scam is news that everyone has read in the print media or heard in the electronic mode. Some of the media reports may not be strictly correct. But issues like arrests and jail terms are facts that cannot be disputed. It surely is a damper when one sees the leading light of an Industry being incarcerated.

Recently I came across a news report of one Indian American Vikram Dutta being arrested by the DEA of the US for drug money laundering. It really shook me up. Doing drugs is bad enough. Being actively involved in the trade with the Colombian mafia is quite another.

I keep asking as to what length we should go to make money. Again in recent times the media reports name quite a number of Indians in the US being investigated and some sentenced to prison terms. I am still not clear as to why educated people having migrated to foreign shores should take up a line of work that contravenes the law of the land. I also wonder in such cases what happens to their families.

News of such misdemeanors over shadow

the wonderful path breaking work carried out by people like Sabir Bhatia, Sam Pitroda and many others. It not only makes us proud, it has helped create a favorable disposition of the Native Americans towards the Indian community. Another example is the Gujarati community[43] who are known for their diligence in setting up and running small business in nearly all geographical areas of the US and the globe.

Need to Change Mind-Set

How many times you must have heard this line. It is a mantra that keeps repeating itself in every sphere of our lives. But its repeated use has had precious little effect in our lives. Probably it has been used too often and by people who did not have the necessary moral quality to use it.

In 2011 one of the teams I have been mentoring won the MIT TR-35 challenge. The process of participation and subsequent evaluation is pretty rigorous. The organizers take pains in verifying the submissions and get in touch with people whose names the applicants give as referees. The entire process takes a few months and culminates in a fanfare gathering along with Indian and American experts.

My team on winning the award was flooded with invitations from various forums

[43] 70% Gujaratis comprises the Indian diaspora.

including business and technology schools, NGOs, Associations of Business and Industry. This was a very grand *tamasha* trying to show case the winners and thus promote a scenario of 'reaching out'.

I have nothing against such a program. All I want to emphasize that a Challenge such as TR-35 highlights only 3 such teams. There are other equally good teams across the country that either have not participated or that they could not qualify in the particular year. If, all those who today invite only the winners of a high profile competition for some felicitations, why is it that they do not take the same initiative as TR-35 undertakes each year? And this can be done state wise, city wise or district wise. It will help create the right eco-system in driving knowledge economy.

I was a member of the Association of Incubators in India. In 2008 I had suggested that the annual meet that the association organizes must be much more meaningful. I am fond of using the word 'deliverable'. Therefore in one of our meeting I asked my colleagues what was the deliverable of this annual meet besides the various sessions spread over two and half days. Actually after having attended such meets both in India and overseas, I find from the first day post lunch sessions the attendance tend to drop. Finally on the 3rd day when the conference actually winds up around tea the participants are down to a minimum. Generally it is the organisers who are still there.

This is not to say that such conferences have no meaningful purpose. The active participants do network. But there are a number who are on the fringes as probably they are the first timers or would like to network with the active members but hardly find the right approach.

I suggested that we run a competition for the incubates of the incubators. And I was entrusted with the task. Now, it is not easy. We had some 35 incubators and even with some 5 teams participating from each of them the number of proposals would be 175.

First I set up a small committee of 3 members. We then formulated the points that would go into the rules of the competition. The competition details were mailed to all the incubators. There were numerous queries over the phone that had to be attended to. By such time, the committee met to decide the names of the jury members. Earlier it was suggested that a few of us would be in the jury. I shot down the proposal. The names of the jurors were kept confidential.

We finally received some 70 entries. It was quite in variance to the original figure of 175. The three member committee scanned the entries to see whether they met the criteria as per the competition rule. I think we rejected five of the proposal. The proposals were then sent to each jury member depending on their area of expertise – Biotech, IT,

Engineering, Agritech, and Green Tech. Sometime in December 2008 we invited all the jury members from across the country to Delhi, where the final selections were carried out. The result of the competition was not divulged and a formal announcement was made only on the final day of the conference.

First, the entire exercise was spread over six months. Secondly, our jury members, each an expert in their own fields, were very cooperative. Third the jury member we had selected to chair the deliberations was a technocrat of eminence. In spite of some urgent engagement he made time for the deliberations. Arising out of this exercise we found our final day session at the conference to be packed to capacity and the media was present too. Needless to say the committee was full of praise for my efforts. I must admit few committees show their trust in one man in organizing such an award. I was free to take my decisions without any hindrances.

Do we seriously want to see Indian startups leap frog into the global arena? Let us seriously put a mechanism in place, first.

3 BUILDING ENTERPRISE

- Create Trust
- At the same keep your eyes open. The previous chapter details some of the issues that an entrepreneur may face.
- Education will always be of help

Be Proud of Your Venture

My entrepreneurial venture started as a distributor of electronic products way back in1972. I was supposed to handle the territory of east India. I set up shop in Kolkata.

I used to get offers for distributing other electronic products such as voltage stabilizers, battery eliminator, battery chargers and emergency lights, most of which were manufactured by local units in and around Kolkata.

Unfortunately, most of the products so offered were of very poor quality. The people behind the enterprise had very little technical competence. A business house based in Kolkata diversified into electronics and started manufacturing voltage stabilizers. These were the "steps up" and "step down" types, using electro-mechanical relays. One of my batch mates at the university requested me to join his company for distributing the product. I did join the company since he knew nothing about distribution, dealer networks, logistics, pricing, dealer margin, support services etc. I asked him to concentrate on the quality assurance of the product that we intended to test market.

This was of paramount importance as the fitters in the assembly line were still learning the ropes. In a few products we found the voltage being boosted where it ought to be reduced. Thus if the input voltage rose to 235V, the faulty stabilizer would increase it to 275V. Obviously, such a situation would critically damage the main equipment.

After some months, I dissociated from the company. I was not in sync with the policy decision of my partner. I did not want any argument as I knew him for a pretty long time and we were friends for long.

However, we kept in touch. A few years down the line, I was told that he had faced a lot of flak from customers whose refrigerators fitted with the voltage stabilizer, suffered major breakdown issues. In some cases, he had to compensate a few of the customers.

India did not have a consumer forum in

those days. Filing a legal suit was cumbersome and expensive. However, soon his sales started falling and he lost the territory rights for the product.

Not only did his business fail, his principle also took a major blow. Few companies have ever recovered from drop in market sales. Once a product loses customer confidence, getting it back is a monumental task.

In recent times, we are seeing a similar phenomenon in the public anger against Wall Street executive in the US and other developed countries. Trust is not built in one day. But trust built over years can be lost in a single day.

In the first two years of my business venture, I lost 80% of my ego. Mumbai was not Kolkata. By the 1970s there were some great innovative startups[44]. Most of the business

[44] Quite a few of them were from the Gujarati community that had fled the Bengal environment where they were in business for a couple of decades. Kolkata in the 50s & 60s was famous for its Chinese eateries. I remember going to Chinese eateries in Mumbai where once the stewards hearing me speak in Bengali, would come and tell his cup full of woes. These Chinese in days to come made a name for their eateries and one of them set up the famous China Garden a top notch Chinese eatery in Mumbai. What Mumbai gained was at the cost

people, though without exemplary educational backgrounds, were actually super businessmen. These kind gentlemen helped me in re-inventing myself. Of course, at times, my ego did play up. My mentor helped in keeping it in check.

I also learnt that one must take pride in his work. One need not be a manufacturer of cars or aircrafts to have such a pride. I was friendly with a person who made various types of plastic parts, small ones (Using mechanical hand press), and generally used in toys. Every time he would design a new item, he would put it in his pocket and bring it over to me for my comment. I understood very little of plastic. Even today I don't. Gradually, I realized that he wanted to share his joy in whatever creativity he was involved. I think it is the crux of any business. Today, I realize such pride leads to lasting joy and a successful venture.

What can a good education do?

We at the factory wanted a printed circuit board (PCB), the kind you see in your computers now, having a certain set of specifications. When we put forward our request, the supplier was flummoxed. All he said was that he can etch it on a glass epoxy board. But that was pretty expensive. Ours were phenolic boards. After a lot of confabulation, I realized that the guy had no clue. Next day, I got back to him asking him whether he could get hold of a hand book on

---

of Kolkata.

printed circuit boards.

He called back after sometime saying he has found a book, but it cost Rs.5000(this was 1973; in those days you could still rent a two room apartment at the plush suburb of Vile Parle, Bombay for Rs. 600 a month). It was a lot of money, yet he was ready to buy it. I told him not to. I went to the book shop[45] and took a look. I found what I needed in just three pages of a 2000-page book. I noted the salient features and we tried it out in his factory. This was the first time I had ever visited a PCB factory.

The process as described in the book was cumbersome. Our labor culminated in some improvements, but not what we needed. However, two things impressed me. First, the inherent willingness of the entrepreneur to learn from a greenhorn. Secondly, when I expressed my disappointment at the result and expressed my regret in putting him through this exercise, the guy consoled me by saying that there was one very important take-home for his manufacturing process.

The guy was a PCB manufacturer[46] from the time I had just entered college. He was established and reputed in his business. Yet,

[45] The shop was Colaba Causeway Bookshop (I hope I got the name right)

[46]A qualified commercial artist from the J J School of Arts

he had no ego in learning the trick of his trade from some unknown entity like me, who read up a few pages of a book a couple of days ago. That was the take-home for me.

And, as a bonus, he took me out for dinner that same evening. Well, you win some and lose some. However, at the end of the day, you start reflecting on your wins that could get you ahead. One must take a quiet pride in his achievements, and keep the ego in tight leash.

7 BUSINESS CONSULTANTS

Businesses need consultants. These people are not paid staff. They charge a fee.

A small and medium sized company definitely needs a sales tax and income tax practitioner on a contractual basis. At times, the company may need a publicity agent, an event manager and sometimes even marketing consultants. Why consultants?

One of the most unflattering comments about consultants I had heard of was that a *consultant* is a guy who tells the time of the day, looking at your watch and submits a bill for his pronouncement.

I used to have numerous run in with the marketing consultant that our company had engaged. I realize today that a consultant is also a very good marketing guy, who normally has an excellent gift of the gab. Thus his advice needs to be sifted through. Some pieces would work well; the others go into the bin.

One has to also remember that if the guy was all that good, he would have a business of his own. The fact that he doesn't proves that he is good only in parts. If entrepreneurs take some pains to work closely with the consultants, a few of them may really be assets for the companies. As consultants work for a number of companies, they can be an excellent source for network building.

Over a period of say three to five years, a competent in house team must be established. These are the three critical areas that I want to mention.

- Technology
- Finance
- Markets and networks.

With a slew of 'knowledge driven' ventures, technology is a critical under belly of any startup. I find a large number of startups enter business with a knowledge bank they already have garnered in their previous assignment. I am not getting into how good the technology is. Many entrepreneurs have started a business with the experience they have gathered in a job with a fairly large company. There are two serious drawbacks in this approach. First, after leaving the job, the inputs freeze. There is an apparent 'stalemate'. This is, however, replenished by the use of Google. Secondly, most of these young startups have worked in line function areas and not in a managerial decision making positions. However, business is the "art of getting to the desired goal, through the expertise of other people." Reflect on it. Can a team of three persons, with very limited resources, crack a competitive market? Yes, provided they acquire the skills in identifying people who can fill in their gaps.

A product or service today would have a

shelf life of not more than three years. So there is a need to start identifying products/services that would be the main stay of the company four years down the line. Yes, it is a tough call. Knowledge enterprises have low shelf life. This is why it is extremely important to create in house competency of people in technology and markets.

Is the Technology chap an omnipotent guy who pulls an application technology out of his hat as and when needed?

No. He is competent in identifying the person for a particular product that the company's marketing guy suggests the company must be able to launch.

This is the name of the game of knowledge enterprise.

We all carry out a SWOT analysis. I am yet to come across a startup that has carried out a SWOT analysis on the company's *chances* in surviving in the market for a fixed period of time. I know people would come back and tell me that any SWOT analysis would give that information.

I disagree. While the current SWOT is needed, it is important to gather information on startups in your regions that are functioning and those that went out of business in the last five years. If you are in Bangalore, try the city region alone. How do you get the information? You can approach the Registrar of Companies where all private limited companies have registered and ask for balance sheets of those firms for the last five years.

Ask your finance guy to study some 50 companies and come up with his conclusion of the matter. A proper analysis can give definite pointers.

Is there any alchemist who can ensure the success of a venture?

Even after 40 years as an entrepreneur I cannot predict. Neither can my close business associates of all sizes. However, one thing that has remained in the back of my mind for these years was the admonition of my family members that I have very little chance of success as I do not come from a business family.

However, I did succeed!

8 KEEP IT SIMPLE

Have you seen the Olympic 'diving' team in action? It is phenomenal. It is so 'cool'. I remember every step of the swimmer, climbing up to the diving platform, walking right to the edge, taking a look at the water down below and steady before leaving the platform in a sculptured pose and knifes into the water below. It always takes my breath away.

My fray in trying some dives from much

lesser heights, were to say the least, unpleasant. I had aches and pain that lasted quite a few days. I understand that it is imperative that the head hits the water along with the entire body at a perfect 90 degrees. If not, it would be a poor dive and a very painful one.

A swimmer who trains to dive has to check out quite a few things. First and foremost his own physical fitness, the depth of the water, whether there are any obstacles down there that could hurt, and the quality of the spring board and of course his own training schedule. Without rigorous training a dive could go horribly wrong.

An entrepreneur is very similar to a swimmer who wants to master his diving skills. He must remember that once he leaves the safety of the diving board, there are no safety nets that could help him in any way, till he hits the water below. The few seconds of fall from the board to the water can make or break him as a champion.

Yes, business plans must be rigorous in its structure. Money must be found to finance the venture; technology is needed to drive the product or services on offer. Yet, the proof of the pudding is the ultimate acceptability of the product/services by the intended buyers. It is the crucial element alone that decides whether the business is a success or a failure.

Just as the diver trains long and hard for a sport that lasts just a few seconds, the entrepreneur needs to interact with potential customers. In doing so, a sample target audience needs to be provided with the product or services and their response to the same need to be closely monitored.

What should be the time span of such a monitoring process? It all depends on when the entrepreneur gets the feel that he has all the data he was looking for so as to take the plunge in enterprise building.

Over the years, I have noticed that entrepreneur either lose patience and form their own opinion or they get side tracked into various related / unrelated issues.

One such issue is VC funding[47]. It is a great paradox; VCs never fund companies that are on the drawing board. Neither do they fund companies that are just about crawling. Therefore, the need for independently identifying what makes the market tick is of prime importance.

Do we seriously want to see Indian startups leap frog into the global arena? What is the mechanism that needs to be in place?

This book is for the entrepreneurs and for those who are toying with the idea of branching out on their own after a few years

[47] As I have mentioned earlier a Fund manager helps out with the market too, that is, provided they agree to fund.

in a job. It is extremely important that they structure their enterprise on the Global Best Practice model, even though they would be operating in India to start with. That is exactly what Flipkart, the Indian online store, has done. Already Indian manufacturers are complaining about Chinese products in the Indian markets. What is the point? One needs to strategize before the commercial launch. Read the market place.

I know you do have a business plan. But has the detailed plan taken care of the multiple issues that you now face? Were you diligent while preparing the plan? Are you tweaking the plan as you go ahead?

I have been a judge in two leading global Challenges. One is as recent as February 2013. I have mentored the teams that won the Social Entrepreneurship Challenge 2011 and the Lockheed Martin Challenge 2011.

These challenges are not something one does for an Academic Project work. Neither are they judged by a few teachers[48]. Normally the

---

[48] At Berkeley I had a long chat with the mentor of the team that won the competition. The team represented the Technical University Munich, one of the foremost technical institutes in the world. He said that it took him the better part of the previous night in trying to convince the leader of the team to tone down the technology component and deal with the business and social relevance. I just hope that today the company is following the dictum.

panel of judges comprises of distinguished VC fund managers, serial entrepreneurs and such academic members who are presently seriously involved with collaborative research with leading industries. A particular judge may differ with the conclusion of the other. But I found that a broad consensus is always there. During the Berkeley Challenge, all judges had gathered in the late afternoon to score the teams. I was for a particular team to be the champion. But a few others were for another team which was also very competent both in their BP and the excellent presentation.

Ultimately we had to go for balloting and the team I had selected lost by 4-6. A very close call. However the same team that lost the first place was unanimously voted as the second best. That is how competitive the top class challenges are.

Questions by the judges usually bring clarity to what has been presented. However, it also at times highlights the deficiencies of the team. Therefore a plan needs to be nitpicked by a set of independent persons before being presented to a VC. I had some unpleasant experience when the team members were upset at my comments on their presentation. I wish they had seen the body language of the top VCs[49] at Berkeley when they put

---

Technology is an enabler which will keep upgrading as time progresses.

questions to the presenter.

Again in 2011 December I was invited by Acara Institute, University of Minnesota, USA to be a judge for their pre-final rounds. The entire judging process and the presentations by combined US + Indian teams were online. Quite a few presentations needed major changes. The Institute had structured the challenge in such a manner that judges were asked to write out comments and send it to them immediately after the presentations. There was also a tabulated format by which we scored the participants.

I was again requested in January 2012 to be the judge for the finals to be held in February. I found to my pleasant surprise that the some of the teams who made it to the finals had actually incorporated the views of the judges in the pre-final rounds. One team in particular did nothing of the sort. May be their mentor advised them accordingly. I don't know. Unfortunately the final results found them out of the race. A

---

[49] Since it was the first time as a judge at a top notch Challenge, I was amused when the Berkeley coordinator requested the VCs to be a bit soft with the teams. I could not understand the relevance as in India our questions to the presenter is pretty banal. Thus when I was invited as a judge for the Acara Institute, University of Minnesota my questions were far more incisive. Berkeley Challenge had been a great learning curve for me.

subsequent comment from the coordinator clearly mentioned the matter of the team ignoring the recommendations of the judges. I wish I can find out as to why they did what they did.

A Plan presentation at a top class platform is not an exam. It is true that many teams participate from academic institutions. The candidate in an exam may get an opportunity in rewriting his paper, or doing far better in the next exam. But a BP generally is a business proposal whereby financiers try and identify teams for funding. If one loses then no funds are forth coming. It is a serious foray in building one's career as an entrepreneur.

The team that was voted as the best at the Acara Challenge, in their presentation made one very significant point – ***'This is a very simple idea'***. We need simple, down to earth ideas to create a successful venture. The fact that the entrepreneurs claimed the idea to be 'simple' reflects the in-depth thought and planning that had gone into it. Not only was the Plan excellent, while reading the proposal I could make an instant connect with the presenter. Once a startup can reach such a stage of simplicity, I will stick my neck out and pronounce that the scheme will be a success.

In this book at various places I have cautioned the startups to be wary in stressing too much on the technology[50] that is the enabler of the enterprise. The simple business that I mentioned in the preceding paragraph uses quite a bit of 'cutting-edge-technology'. It needs the technology to drive the business. Unfortunately I am not in a position to elaborate for obvious reasons.

Why is it that large numbers of technology startups get lost in their self-created maze? Frankly, I have no answer. Obviously a techie team comprises of people with average plus intelligence. I can in bits and pieces try and find some reasons for such predicament. One I have already mentioned in the book is the mode of technical education in the country. Having said that, how can intelligent youngsters shut themselves up in their rooms and be oblivious of their eco-system?

---

[50] I started my career as a developer of linear integrated circuits used in high fidelity audio systems. This was 1970 April/May. I developed the Baxandall equalizer for the amplifier which till then was not used in any Indian amplifiers. At the same time I incorporated various external control systems so that the user could use the amplifier semi-professionally. I was told by my marketing group that such devices will confuse the user and asked me not to incorporate the same. I was absolutely disheartened. Initially I tried to reason. It did not work. Looking back I think I was wrong in my approach. The customer needs a very user friend product.

9 THE DISCONNECT

From 1998 till 2010 I have been involved in establishing academic incubators in leading academic institutions in the country. In this period I have conducted innumerable seminars, workshops and skill set training programs. The participants ranged from educated farmers, undergraduates, Graduate students and professionals including startups. Most of the students came from the best institutions of the country (usually from the East). A sort of crème-de-la-crème of the student community. After a couple of years I found to my dismay the following that I have appended.

Students were only interested in obtaining a certificate. The first year under grad students lost interest as early as the second year! From the second year onwards they were into preparation of various entrance exams – management, chartered accountancy, GRE, and similar. In the Indian academic system entrepreneurial workshops, seminars and Business Plans do not carry any meaningful value.

Their teachers dissuaded them from participating in any entrepreneurship related programs. Instead they were encouraged to apply for post graduate programs of their choice at any university and subsequently for their doctoral program.

I could filter out just two students who continued with my program. They had landed excellent jobs immediately after their graduation. Mckinsey picked up one of the college students Swati Bagaria. One day she came up to me and handed the note. I was touched. I am reproducing the letter[51]. The other Dhrupad Raja a Commerce graduate gave up his plans to travel to the US and started an agri-tech company. Unfortunately the institutions gave no publicity to this. Academic institutions in India feel comfortable in following the beaten path – chalk and talk.

One day another student came to thank me for the programs he had attended. He was the only student who was successful in gaining admission to IIM Calcutta that year (2005) from the college.

Much later I had organized an advanced program for post graduate students in life sciences in collaboration with the post graduate department of the University of Kolkata. The participants handed me a 'thank you' letter that I have taken the liberty in appending here[52]. Interestingly, the pro-vice –chancellor was also present at the presentation.

This was surely an achievement. But if I look at the number of students (1500) and the

---

[51] Annexure

[52] Annexure

numbers that benefitted from the initiative, I feel disheartened. We speak of Excellence. I wonder whether Excellence is defined as per a location, a person or a region. We do not hesitate to mention global. Yet in our actions we are so conservative.

I wondered as to where had I gone wrong? I looked carefully at the structure of my programs and suddenly one day realized that these programs were meant for knowledge startups and those who intend to become startups. Earlier what I tried to do was similar to taking the horse for a drink. I could not make the horse drink.

In a sense it was a 'brick wall' in my endeavor in creating an entrepreneurial mindset amongst students, especially those who enroll for the Degree college programs. One must remember that the country has thousands of degree colleges with a few million students. In 2003 when I had shifted from IIT to a degree college in Kolkata, my primary objective was to create this entrepreneurial attitude in a reasonably good degree college. Mind you, this was way before the famous utterances by industry spokesperson saying that technology graduates were unemployable. In India, barring a handful of degree colleges that are most sought after[53],

[53] Though the colleges have a reputation, there are no guarantees for a job. Most of these institutions have a placement cell that is dormant. As an example, in 2004-05 one such

the rest has questionable standards of education. Technology institutions on the other hand are better regulated and numbers of technology institutions are much less than degree colleges. If Industry is dismissive of technology graduates, what about those graduating with just a general B.A. or B.Sc. degree?

But as I had mentioned earlier it was not to be. The faculty members were uncooperative. I changed track and started interviewing and selecting people from all walks of life. In the process, I did select a few students, too but not necessarily from the college where I had established the center.

My NGO network and Agriculture Development Officers of the state government helped me in identifying suitable candidates from rural India. I have found that the rural areas are bereft of some very ordinary facilities that people in the city never give a second thought. For example, we are so used to 24 hour water on the tap. This is unheard of in rural areas. I also found that the rural youth are far sincere in their approach to a program and extremely street smart that helped me to raise the bar of my programs. The only drawback was their lack of comprehension in English.

I quickly changed the medium of instruction to the local language. At the same time I introduced a few session in conversational

---

college with a strength of 1500 students claimed to have placed 192.

English. Having also worked in Odisha, I must admit that Bengal is far better in English comprehension.

One of the many programs I want to highlight is a month long skill set training program in Agri-tech Business. The basic program was divided in two distinct categories – 10 days at a R&D lab for training in basic plant biotechnology, 4 days in the field and another 15 days management program designed for such startups. After this program we proposed that the participants go back to their place of residence and work on a 'practical' business plan. Organizing faculty for all this took no time as I knew most leading experts personally. They helped in designing the curriculum, too.

Next was the selection of participants. I selected a mix. They were entrepreneurial students, existing entrepreneurs and entrepreneurs from rural areas. The last group comprised nearly 40% of the total. My idea was that besides the training we impart everyone would have something to learn from each other as the entire program was residential.

At the outset when I found that there was a serious problem of communication by the rural group. I realized this urban ambience had a part to play in their reticence. In trying to assimilate this group into a homogeneous one, I appointed two senior entrepreneurs as coordinators of the team.

I had to do a fair amount of juggling with my budget. Each participant had paid R5000/- . It hardly covers the cost of board and lodging in a city for an entire month. But even today R5000/- is a fair sum in rural Bengal. I wanted the participants to appreciate that there was more than enough 'bang' for the money they had paid.

At the valedictory, I was pleased that besides the participants, the faculty and NGOs who had helped were present. I started the proceedings telling the gathering that as organizers we would like to hear about their experience, good and bad. Even if it was bad they ought not to worry in narrating it as the month long workshop was over. It was a very pleasant surprise that each member of the rural group was very articulate in his/her views. I wondered, if we could make such a difference in a month, an extended training can create *magic.*

At the end of the valedictory I announced that we had decided to award cash prizes to the first two teams. Needless to state that the teams presented excellent business plans. An entrepreneur with a running enterprise won the first prize. But one cannot grudge him as his plan was by far superior.

I think being an entrepreneur helped me to read the ground realities and accordingly devise such programs[54].

---

[54] There was one discordant note. One of the

After the success of the last program, I spread my net wider and invited participants from the Eastern Region.

Well in a way I raised the bar again. I wanted graduates in Life Sciences or Agriculture who were already in some entrepreneurial activities. To make this program successful individual attention need to be given. I had decided that not more than 10 participants should be inducted. However, with the rush of applicants from states like Nagaland, Mizoram, Odisha the number went up to 13. At the very end I received a request from two girl candidates in biotechnology from Odisha. I have always tried to accommodate women. In this particular case there was a problem as I had no accommodation for lady candidates. I requested the university to accommodate them in their hostel. The university had rented some apartments for female students. They agreed. However, one day I received a call from my office that the guardian accompanying the female participants was appalled seeing the hostel. I was on the phone and wondering whether I have to ultimately deny them participation in the program. Again I thought that they had

CEOs of a NGO I had invited to judge the final presentation after having his share of the refreshments, asked the servers to pack some for him which he carried back. None of the participants made such a request. ***We learn from such incidents every day***.

taken the trouble in traveling all the way from Odisha. They were serious. I told my assistant to accompany them to my residence. In the meantime I called my wife and asked her to allow the students to occupy the first floor fully furnished apartment in my building. I have a few apartments unoccupied in my house. Fortunately the guardian who had accompanied these two participants was mighty pleased once he saw it[55].

For a couple of sessions we had invited the star performer of my previous workshops. That was a pretty informal interaction and I was happy to note that all the participants were pretty comfortable asking questions and discussing the issues raised. It was one entrepreneur to the other. The last such session I had organized was in 2009. Till date, three of the participants have kept in touch. We need a network of entrepreneurs to create an eco-system that in turn will help motivate and drive other budding enterprises. This network will help grow the entrepreneurial talent too. No amount of classroom teaching can achieve what a network can do.

In a city where the university has no campus, facilities for housing participants for short duration is a major problem[56]. We could not

[55] I am yet to comprehend how senior officials at the university glibly told me that accommodation was not a problem. Or was it my lack of insight in realizing what was actually on offer.

keep them at locations far away as they have no idea of the city and the local transport. It was not possible to organize a pickup and drop every day. Transport costs in cities are prohibitive and our participation fee was nominal. The sessions were held at our premises where we had all the necessary facilities and AV aids. It took sometime but once such matters were resolved everything went as clockwork. The other issue was that incubators have the bare minimum support staff. All of us needed to be hands on. I must admit that my staff was very cooperative and never complained or ever took leave under any pretext. But establishing any new institution like an incubator which in any case was the first such in the state, meant that my staff had no idea as to what is expected from them. Fortunately they carried out to the T whatever I asked them to do. During the preparatory phase all of us used to be in office for 12+ hours. Since my institution was a government organization, the rules did not allow me to pay extra for the extra hours

---

[56] We had additional grants for the program that was carried out earlier on. I had organized the workshop from the incubator of another institution I was heading. This was at a fairly new incubator of a recently established state university. The university as I have mentioned did not have a campus at that point and it was housed in a three storied building with very limited space for the university to function smoothly.

they put in. The most I could do was to pay them a tiffin allowance and some money for their transport. I wish we have a system to reward the sincere workers.

Earlier I had mentioned 2009 was the last major workshop[57] I had organized, I had also supported a major program in Natural Dye making and textile printing as part of skill set training for the indigenous weaver of Bengal at Ushagram in Nadia district of West Bengal.

The organizing part was carried out by the NGO located at the place. Faculty was provided by another NGO. I stepped in to see to it that they have some of the best people in the country to do the training. Since the place was a 4 hour drive from the city, I could manage to go there for the valedictory. I was taken in by the enthusiasm of the participants who were either weavers and/or designers. During an interaction on

[57] My next two assignments were at institutions where they had no clue as to how to go about the matter. The people assigned to me for support were inefficient to say the least. I tried my level best. One program that I literally forced the institution to carry out ended in a disaster. After we had reached our destination, we found the place locked. After waiting for half an hour someone came to tell us that my institution had not given him any prior intimation. My people started arguing. What was the point? I stopped that heated talk and came away.

the subject of marketing I found two women in the mid-20s who had done their graduation degree, savvy. I believe with the present setup, a considerable amount of inputs can be provided to people who are already in the trade. Our foray in identifying and training people in skill set is an extremely arduous task. Maybe somebody will come forth with easily implementable programs in future.

Every skill set program is domain specific. For the weavers we had to get hold of a good designer. This was crucial as natural dyes normally give a dull appearance when they are used on cotton. We identified a designer from National Institute of Design, Ahmedabad, who agreed to be stationed in Kolkata for nearly a month. One of the reasons why a program requires a lot of attention at the formative stages is owing to the critical components being in place. If we miss out any one component, the program falls flat.

Ushagram, the place where the program was conducted, has an extensive campus established by a dedicated school teacher. After his retirement he had donated all his savings to the NGO and started living there. When I met him on the day, I found him in a room which was 10X10 ft. and very spartan. At the time he was nearly 90 years old. I walked around the complex. They help the local community in various ways including packaging spices as per European standards and exporting them. I was quite impressed as European food laws are extremely stringent and their quality standards for organic produce pretty difficult to achieve in our country as because most of the topsoil of the land where plants are grown have been contaminated by some chemical or other. Most of the growers have been using chemical fertilizer and chemical insecticides for long many years. The process of cleaning the top layer is tedious and expensive. Further one must have a certificate from an approved EU agency certifying the soil contamination free. Few players in India have gone ahead and done so. The fact that Ushagram is one of them made me happy.

As I have again and again stressed that the entire program in changing mind-sets to go global depends on the person or persons who take it upon themselves to drive such initiatives. Needless to state one never knows what will succeed. But the passion cannot diminish. Many a times it is a thankless job. But, one do not look at such enterprise as 'job'.

Around the same time I was requested by the Department of Science and Technology, Government of West Bengal to accompany a team who was going to visit the B. B. College at Asansol[58]. I was not too keen, as even if I would have liked to support an activity there, I do not have the logistic to handle such a

[58] Asansol is a town which is a 3 hour train ride from Kolkata. It used to be a mining town. Today it is a bustling business centre.

program.

Since the officer heading the government team was a close friend, I agreed to go. Let me first give you a firsthand glimpse of the college. The college is located on a by-lane of the town. It is a very ordinary looking 3-storied building (I hope my memory serves me right). There was an Annex to the main building where on the ground floor the principal had his office. The principal's office was just a tiny room.

But what caught my eye was the fact that the faculty has been conducting experiments in bio-diesel for some years and their vehicle was being run on bio-fuel. The bio-fuel was extracted from Jatropa nuts. The college had designed and installed such an extraction unit on its premises. They were also extracting citronella oil which they were selling to a few pharma and cosmetic companies. In all my years at Kolkata I have only heard some teachers extolling others to be engaged in various productive activities but this was the first time I actually saw the teachers leading the project. Surely I was taken aback. I realized this was not some ordinary college. I felt exhilarated speaking to the faculty members each of whom had a vision. Later in the day I sat down with the principal and enquired about the Academic programs. The college conducts under graduate and post graduate programs in nearly all disciplines. It was in the process of obtaining permission from the University for conducting Ph.D.

programs. The college has a NAAC[59] 'A' accreditation. I remember once back in the city, I had met the principal of the college where I had my center and narrated the incident. He had never heard the name of the college. Colleges in the city once they received the 'A' rank have organized press conferences and what not. But a *mofussil* college in the same state having similar or better teaching standards goes un-noticed. I wish when I had moved out of IIT, Kharagpur, somebody had mentioned the name of B.B. College. It would have been an ideal place in the state for my venture. Creating the entrepreneurial eco-system is indeed a difficult task. Promoting the idea of entrepreneurship can only follow when you have the eco-system in place.

10 ENTREPRENEURS AND THE ECO-SYSTEM

[59] NAAC – National Assessment and Accreditation Council an autonomous body of the University grants Commission of the Govt. of India. How does a rating 'A' rank amongst other colleges in Bengal. To the best of my knowledge some of the top reputed colleges are A. Only 3 colleges have been ranked as A+. What this does not mean, and I would surely like to clarify, all reputed colleges are not necessarily A, they could have lower ranking.

The first 20 years of my entrepreneurial ventures I had spent in Mumbai. Mumbai is the commercial capital of the country. By and large it is the Gujarati community who rule the business in the city. I remember the initial years there very well. Wherever I went to meet someone at his business place, the concerned person will surely ask ***'suu dhandho karocho'***, which translate as what business are you in. This is in contrast to people in Bengal where one will be asked, where do you work. The Mumbai businessman loses interest in you if you say you are an employee. He will then call a subordinate and ask him to deal with you. In Kolkata if one says he is in business the other guy loses interest[60]. Do you realize how difficult it is to create the environment conducive for entrepreneurs to grow in Bengal and generally in the Eastern region?

The other things I realized after spending 4 of the 6 years I ran the incubators in the city, that the majority that lives in rural Bengal are far more enterprising than the Kolkata 'babus'. The small town and villages have no

[60] It seems that the word 'babu' evolved in Bengal, signifying clerks in Government services. Bengalis were derided for their babu culture whatever they may signify. I have not tried to find an answer as there are multiple renditions of the word.

comparable facilities that the city has. Not many years back, critically ill patients had to be rushed to some Kolkata hospital. At my clinic it was very common to find ambulances bringing in the sick from places a far as 100 km from Kolkata.

For students coming to Kolkata from outside for studies is no joke. Any accommodation except a college hostel[61] is expensive. I can safely assume that a person residing in the *mofussil* areas has a level of income that is in sync with the local cost of living. How can the person suddenly manage to rent a room in the city unless he is one of the rare moneyed landowners?

In the period I did establish and run the two incubators (2003-2008) some 4000 students had participated in my programs. If you divide the figure by 30 you will get the number of program I had conducted every year. Please keep in mind that the primary objective for an incubator is not to conduct a program. It is to incubate a startup team. Please go through the write up on incubation and startups to get a hang of what needs to be done to successfully incubate startups. Thus in the same period I had mentored some 70 startups. 20 of them are in business till date. But if one sees the total population of the state this figure is not even a drop in this vast population. My initiative was meant to be a precursor of what can be done in teaching institutions. The results would

[61] Getting a seat in a hostel is a matter of pure chance.

follow provided, the same is replicated and upgraded in terms of content and tweaked for local needs, from time to time. I do not think that is happening today.

I tried many avenues. One was an informal round table for students. I wanted the students, from any discipline to come forth for an hour or so once a week and have a chat with their fellow students over a cup of tea and some snacks. We provided the eats. It worked for 3 months and folded. As I had mentioned earlier, that with a bare minimum support staff carrying out all such activities created a lot of stress. For the first two years my staff members had no clue what they were in for. My office assistant probably thought that she would be there to type and file a few letters and attend to the telephone. The office boy must have thought that his job would be to serve tea to the visitors and keep the office clean. But in the two years I trained both of them to man a seminar and a workshop, organize data sheets for the participants, set up audio visual aids, and attend to enquiries and to handle cash and keep accounts. Simultaneously I trained them in attending to the back office requirements of my startups. In 2009 January my office assistant migrated to the UK. I understand she has a decent job in an office. At the end as the saying goes – The operation was successful but the patient died. The entrepreneurial set up has all but folded up.

11 STRUCTURE OF INCUBATION

I have mentioned earlier in my book that it is the government of India that has taken an initiative in driving the entrepreneurship[62]

---

[62] Some NGOs across the country do supplement efforts of the farmers in the rural

program. I have summarized a few of the issues.

The bureaucrats decide which institution needs support.

The responsibilities in the execution of the program rest on the institution.

Hardly any academic institution has an entrepreneurial eco-system. Neither do they have any interaction with Industries through joint research programs[63].

---

areas. But the institution of academic excellence as established by the Nobel Laureate Tagore at Shantiniketan, a very private initiative, has no parallel. The Sabarmati Ashram in Ahmadabad by the Mahatma is another notable institution that in its period brought to the fore through its activities of spinning the chakra, the pride in being an Indian and giving a value to Indian product by shunning foreign goods, a movement that Gandhi had nurtured. There would be no point in having such a movement without showing the people of the country how they could on their own procure the essential necessities with indigenous resources. Something similar is missing in all present government programs.

[63] A very small percentage of academic institutions have full-fledged in-house research facilities and programs in place.

The academic institutions are all autonomous and answerable only to their boards.

In all the 6 incubators I have established I found the administrators waiting for the grant money[64]. Not even in a single case have they started the program while the other processes are on. An incubation program is not a degree course, where there is starting date and a finish. I feel that academic institutions lack commitment. But since the grant amount is relatively high, they tend to play along.

Once the grant money comes in a process is somehow started. How can the process be started if faculty in charge of the incubator has not been suitably trained?[65]

There are no annual published reports of incubators where money has been sanctioned. I don't think anyone is actually aware of what is really happening and how the money has actually been utilized.

In the past 3 years the government in addition to giving such grants has also provided incubators' with additional funds.

Not one Indian academic institution figures in the first 100 of the global list.

[64] Federal government largesse.

[65] For universities and privately funded autonomous institution an Incubator qualifies for additional points in the NAAC rating.

If an incubator is successful, it is not the government that ought to fund it. The business will come forward and fund it. That is the litmus test. Slowly and surely such federal funding will make this initiative another NREGA[66].

Suddenly a number of ministries joined hands in providing funds. Instead of identifying newer areas and groups these ministries are picking those that have already been identified by the DST for the incubator program. I don't think the academic institutions ever had such delectable windfall.

Instead the need of the hour is a *community funded* incubation program. If some facilitation in terms of funds is provided by the federal government, it ought to evaluate the past 26 years of DST program and set in motion programs that directly help create an eco-system.

I have a very basic question in the primary policy of the government funding of academic incubators. The country is aware of the fact that the quality of education in the country leaves much to be desired. Barring a handful of government funded academic institutions the rest are suffering from poor quality of faculty members, non-standard lab facilities, and library and hostel accommodations for their students. In such a

---

[66] National Rural Employment Guarantee Act

scenario from where will these institutions get people to man incubators? Obviously, incubators are relegated down the line in order of priority.

Many institutions have a fairly large campus. The buildings are also pretty decent. But both land and buildings make economic sense to the promoters of the institution. Attracting capable faculty members with proper academic system in place is another story. Excellence in academics does not directly translate into money. It is like wine from Bordeaux. A good wine takes years to mature. It is the matured stuff that commands a premium. Let us all first be sure whether the present institutions would like to wait for at least a decade before they start raking in the *moolah*.

The government works like a house divided. The Ministry of Science and Technology under which the DST operates, does not bother about academics. The Ministry of Human Resource Development under which the University Grants Commission[67] works, does not oversee the incubation program[68].

---

[67] The government watchdog for Universities and academic institutions in the country. Some of academicians with the UGC are pretty savvy about incubators. But they do not get invited to the DST panel on incubators.

[68] The Incubation Program is supposed to include Intellectual Property Rights, Technology Transfers from Institute R&D to Industry,

Plus when it comes to hard cash, obviously there is no uniformity. I am sure there is also a lobby group at work.

We in India benefitted immensely from the entrepreneurial initiatives in IT enabled Services. Thus today the outsourcing business alone in India directly employs some 3m people (indirect employment 8.9m), all with a certain level of education and a decent salary. Years ago NASSCOM an association of the fledgling software industry was floated. The person credited with building this up was Dewang Mehta[69]. Recognizing the potential of the software and services segment as a major foreign exchange earner, Mehta launched the India Inc.

Royalty payments etc. The role of the academia in its success is critical.

[69]Dewang Mehta (August 10, 1962-12 April 2001) was the head of NASSCOM from 1991 to 2001. He is credited with a large portion of India's momentous rise as a "software giant". – Wikipedia

The period between 1991 and 2001 was one of transformation and growth, for both Nasscom and Mehta. Each drew sustenance from the other. As Mehta grew in stature, gaining respect within the Indian ICT sector as an industry leader, Nasscom too began to evolve into an association of substance. The government remained a silent spectator.

Crusade, where he personally marketed the capability of the Indian software industry to the world.

Unfortunately, Mr. Mehta died young. The association by then had grown in size and also by the combined revenue of its members. The government that was earlier very ambivalent jumped on to the bandwagon. Every state chief minister reached out to establish at least one IT hub. Politically it was the most expedient decision as an IT hub ensures definite employment to the educated youth.

This is precisely what I am driving at. If we need to create an eco-system for Innovation and Entrepreneurship that would someday reach the levels that NASSCOM had reached under Mehta, it must be a passionate initiative of one or more people of the country and not that of any bureaucrat or the bureaucratic rigmarole. My experience says that such initiatives are personality driven. No bureaucrat or a Professor at a University can do it. There is surely a model to follow. Why are we trying to re-invent the wheel? In the process of re-inventing the wheel a large sum of public money is being misused or not efficiently used.

In the years that Dewang Mehta ran round in circles to get this business moving, all the other lead associations of Business and Industry were watching the fun. All these associations are lobby groups and every year the person who becomes the President is expected to cosy up with the government in power. These associations I am talking of are there from the time of independence or even earlier.

Yet in the period 1947-2001 they could not bring forth anything dramatic to change the fortune of the people of the country, which NASSCOM did. Moreover, India which had small and medium manufacturing units pre-independence, lost the manufacturing bus altogether and became large scale importers where the members of these associations are local agent for the overseas companies.

Yes, we keep hearing of wealth in the hands of the few. But even today I do not see any effort by the government to spread the wealth. A number of Indians have salted away their ill-gotten gains in various tax-havens. A list of such depositors is already with the government for the past 4 years. The powers that be have done nothing to bring these wrong doers to book. All the government talks of is various schemes in providing subsidies for the weaker sections of the society. Subsidy, too, is sorely needed to tide over the present. The avenues for creating indigenous economic activities that larger sections of the civil society can participate will ultimately make the program sustainable. Siphoning off funds of the government must stop.

A story of the 60s and 70s was that 2 business houses ran the economy of the country. At the time the population was about 600m. Isn't it ridiculous that so many people were dependent on the whims of just a handful of people for their daily bread?

I remember the Mafatlal House[70] an edifice in South Mumbai was a sort of tourist destination in the early 70s. Yet a decade down the line Mafatlal was out of business. The same was the case of Nirlon, Premier Auto the Khataus and many others. I don't think they became paupers. But the business disappeared. Similar fate befell the monopoly manufacturers of two indigenous cars – Ambassador and Fiat. Why did these business houses fall by the wayside despite the growing car market?

The planners of the government vision document are generally not in sync with the administrators who are in the line function. A media report[71] speaks about the ministry of HRD proposing vocational training programs in schools and colleges. The structure of the program has not been disclosed.

However, the same government a couple of years ago has implemented a program under the National Skill Development Corporation[72] in a PPP mode with the Ministry of finance

[70]A multi-storied office block with climate control, something new in those days.

[71] HT Feb 9, 2012

[72]http://www.nsdcindia.org/about-us/organization-profile.aspx

having 49% equity. Instead of other related ministries joining hands and strengthening the movement which is yet to show any visible result, the others are trying to establish newer facilities that on paper aim to achieve the same results.

When the NSDC was setup the government claimed that the goal of the organization would be to impart skills to 500m people in a period of time. Now it seems that the planners have already given up on NSDC. Nobody has a surefire solution. At least a PPP model delinks such initiative from bureaucrats who are best left to administer in various areas of governance. I wrote this book in 2012. In 2014 when I sat down to review what I had written, I find that the present Prime Minister Modi had focused extensively on skill training during his run up to the elections.

Before India opened up post 1991, we the people, were always dependent on government officials for nearly all aspects of our lives. Getting a passport, which later the courts declared was a basic right of every citizen, was a nightmare. I need not go into those details as it's quite well known. Those who do not understand, please speak to the elders in the family.

Unfortunately the bureaucratic attitude has not changed. It does the system no good when senior officers are arrested for corruption. Probably the silver lining are the young officers like the Collectors of some districts in Odisha, Maharashtra and Jharkhand who risk their lives in visiting the Naxalite affected areas and in the process are abducted. The majority however are still in their old mode of jockeying for power. And the power flows when one is occupying such a chair that has the power to disburse money. Anything else is of no consequence. This is not to say that all such officers are corrupt. But the initiative needed to implement the holistic programs by all such officers is absent. It is the very notion of acting like a satrap that these officials find attractive. You can well comprehend how difficult it is for the abject poor to approach such officials. And as per official figures 30% of the population is 'below the poverty line'.

As you can understand, and it is not because I am writing about it, you will face similar situations too, there is no systemic change. Without such a change the well-meaning policies will come to a naught.

A piquant situation arose when I started the various entrepreneurship programs at the college in Kolkata. Till such time I was at IIT, and the issue never came up in the manner as I am about to narrate.

The students at the college asked me whether the EDC[73] could give them a certificate for the various programs they would be

[73] Entrepreneurship Development Cell (under the scheme of the Department of Science and Technology, Government of India)

participating in. At first I thought that a certificate of completion was in order for the benefit of participants.

However, I checked with DST as to whether other centers give such certificate. I received a very diplomatic response which in effect meant do not give certificates as the UGC frowns on any other body giving certificates. I was in a fix. On one hand the participant who is making an effort to participate needs something to show for the effort, on the other it was a directive.

After some thought, I decided to give a certificate of participation. UGC till date does not certify any vocational program. Yet they have formulated a program for vocational traing. Why such an attitude? An entrepreneurship program follows the guidelines of the DST. Every EDC has a committee of independent experts who oversee these programs. It also helps the candidate in a job interview, as I had narrated the cases of participants in my programs. In both cases they had to communicate what they did in the programs. It is so much easier to show the certificate and then speak about it. The right hand of the government has no clue as to what the left is doing.

12 THE CHALLENGE

- Never bad-mouth competition

Starting an entrepreneurial venture, as you will well understand, is no easy task. You are to expect challenges, in a way, you are supposed to enjoy those challenges. There will always be a brick wall that will try to stop you from your goal. And your job will be to cross that wall. In fact, one must accept that challenges are good. Challenges ensure that only those with the passion, the zeal, will succeed. The rest will have to seek other options. Here I would like to discuss a few challenges, some expected while some unexpected.

Do Not Run Down Your Competitor

Startups keep talking of cutting edge technology of their new products. That is good news. But any technology will sooner than later finds a competitor (as Intel found

AMD). And once there is competition, each technology provider will have a set of its own customers. That is how the market works.

Cosmic was arguably the finest indigenous music system of the '70s till the end of the '80s. But there were others too – a few small guys like us, and a couple of big names[74]. The big names were marketing their music systems using advertisement and publicity blitz. But the product did not in any way match the claims of their fancy ads. Yes, the product was 20% cheaper than ours, but the quality too was 80% poorer. We were small compared to the biggies.

They had marketing set-up in tier II cities. We did not. Those were not the days of mobile phones and internet. One needed an excellent sales force to reach tier II cities. We had none. During one of our brainstorming sessions, quite a few of our team members harped on comparing our products' specifications with those of the competitors using the print media.

I vehemently objected. My reasoning was two-fold. First, our budget was limited. We really could not think of matching the publicity campaign that consists of Point of Sale materials, shop displays, incentives to dealers and salesmen and advertisement in the print media.

[74] Philips and Bush

Secondly, I strongly believed that deriding our competitor is not a good marketing strategy. I would rather like our prospective customer to weigh the options available. I suggested we budget an amount of money that can be used to raise client awareness in identifying the quality of a high fidelity music system. My proposal was appreciated and adopted.

This is just one small aspect of the market dynamics. There are number of others and each instance typical to the needs of a start-up. The majority of books on marketing speak on topics such as market survey, research, pricing, aspects of retailing, etc. Most of such topics are related to financial issues. I have found that start-ups while speaking on marketing would either shift to their financial problems or they want to have an in-depth understanding of branding and advertisement in the print or electronic media. While the former is concerned with finances, the latter has no clue to the financial commitments in following an elaborate path of branding through advertisements using the media.

There is another variant in start-ups. I see a large number of technology driven start-ups. Some use sophisticated 'algos' for software, some are product companies, though product companies are far fewer in numbers. The technology start-ups, I call them 'techies', usually have quite a few innovations on their bench. After one is ready and tested, they tend to move into developing the other. Since start-ups are small team operations, any change in focus is bound to have far reaching effect on the business.

What happens is that once the product is ready, tested and found to be quite 'acceptable', the next move should be making the product 'ready for market'. A product is successful when customers are found. And such 'customers' are those that purchase the product/service. In course of time, they would recommend the product to their friends. If this cycle is broken, the product will stop selling and even if we term it to be a technical success, it just happens to be one of the non-starters. Such a situation is to be avoided as resources in terms of innovative energy and money have been spent in the pre-operations. Techies get upset when I tell them that product development is at most 10% of the business.

Earlier in the book I had mentioned about a technical team that had accessed a fair amount of money through government VC funding. Unfortunately, when they came for advice, the money was all gone and they were on the verge of closing shop.

Managing the Enterprise - People

Turning around a business that has come a cropper owing to mismanagement takes inordinate skill and immense sacrifice from the team. I am yet to meet a team that has done so. Usually the members start blaming one other. Obviously the skill is not available in-house. The team leader needs to take stock and carry out a major shakeup. There needs to be clinical precision. Not only the approach is undesirable, it breaks up the team and some of the positive work done in the past is lost.

I had a person working in the marketing department for a period of five years. It was decided that once I found him competent to handle the particular department in its totality, I shall spin it off as a new company where he would be eligible for 25% of the equity in addition to his salary. This was at a period when Indian business had not heard of employee stock options.

Everything went well. I had him to head my office in Chennai. After about a year, I realised that he was more interested in working in Kolkata. I came to know that in Chennai he was missing his friends. But, he never told me so.

Ultimately, a time came to take a decision and I very politely told him about my inability to offer him a pie of the company in Kolkata. I also asked him to take some time to respond to our discussions. In a span of 10 days he came over to tell me that he would quit. I agree all such separations may not follow such a smooth path. But at the same time it should not turn ugly.

In another instance the separation nearly turned ugly. I had established a business in Kolkata with another person as a 50% equity partner. It was understood that he would contribute in phases towards the equity transferred to him. The amount was decided on the valuation of the property which I held.

After two years, he refused to pay. As the understanding was a verbal[75] one, I had no legal ground to enforce it. This is a very important lesson I learnt. Legal papers must be fool proof. It is the insurance when dispute arises. Till they do arise the paper is just a paper. Once the dispute arises it is the most important insurance.

Well, my partner and I did exchange some unpleasant words; I wish I never did that. He did exit my business after I paid him off. Unfortunately, our association on a personal level, too, came to an end. Looking back, I wish I had handled the matter far more diplomatically.

Is your Business on the Roll?

In business, we often hear from our compatriots, how is your business 'running'?

[75] A lot of business dealing used to be done in India on verbal commitments. Some of the indigenous commercial activities are still carried out on verbal commitments. IP, Patents and related issues are a very recent entrant in the Indian markets, and just like the British, a legacy of the foreigners. I am not saying it is a good or bad development.

The key word 'run' must be kept in mind. First the startups set up the venture. A fair amount of thought goes into product/services, marketing and finance. Once the revenue starts, we can call it a 'running' business provided the revenue generation is continuous. This requires extraordinary skill. Every day in a business is a 'new' day, with new issues and roadblocks.

One of the first companies I mentored in Kolkata was set up by a non-resident Indian. He was not a rookie and was engaged in business in the USA. I understand he did pretty well in the period between 1994 and 1999 (in the US). He did exit just before the Y2K bubble burst.

His business in the US was in the telecom sector. Here in India, in 2003, he found opportunity in BPO training which was a fast growing business, starved of trained manpower. He started training people to man BPOs and call centres. As with all businesses, his initial foray ran into some hiccups. He was an incubate[76] in the incubator at EDC, St. Xavier's College, Kolkata, established by me through a government grant.

In a very short span, his business boomed. He ramped up so fast, that I remember pointing out to him that the business may fall apart. It was like a second hand car with a

[76] An Incubator provides physical facilities for a limited period to startups. A committee decides on the matter. The incumbents are called 'incubates'.

brand new V8 engine but a very shaky chassis on the race track.

But success is heady. It is very difficult to resist money filling the coffers of the company. By 2006, he had moved out of EDC and I had lost track of his business, till one day, over the phone he told me that the business has all but wound up. I was disappointed. Today, I realise that here, in our country, a mentor's guidance is treated just like any advice dished out by all and sundry. And nobody is really interested in advice. A mentor is not a casual advisor. He is a rare expert on the subject of start-ups.

'Business as usual' is a common refrain heard everywhere. But there is no business which is 'usual'. Business is a complex operation which has changing parameters that need to be stabilised on a continual basis.

For example, you walk into your office and find that there is a breakdown in power supply. Well, you got to set it right immediately. Simultaneously, you got to attend to your business priorities of the day. Both require equal attention. You need to bring the power back on, to normalise the office operation. It must be kept in mind that without electrical power, the operations can at best be run for a couple of hours or so. Anything more than that will lead to complications, frayed tempers and total disruption.

This was a simplistic instance[77]. Nowadays consumer laws have become very stringent. One never knows when a disgruntled customer would move the consumer court.

Primary Focus

To guard against such eventualities, the company has to keep a strict watch on the following.

1. Quality
2. Meeting delivery schedules
3. Customer support

Even today, I am not sure why the company incubated at my incubator in Kolkata engaged in training and doing so well suddenly stopped in its track. Over the years some news trickled in about poor customer support, which led to serious dissatisfaction and other legal issues.

[77] I mention power outage as it is the most common phenomenon in the country.

13 VENTURE CAPITAL

Ideally a start-up needs a marketing consultant who, besides having some on-the-job experience, must have been an entrepreneur himself. In today's knowledge-driven enterprise, it is a necessity to evaluate the probable customers. I personally think that landing a VC fund helps as the VC brings in his huge market networks and expertise in working the markets. After all, his money is involved. Probably the VC would be the right bet, besides the money he provides.

But VC/angel funds have a downside. For a successful start-up it would be prudent to exit the firm once it is on the roll rather than work under supervision of a VC. Again this is an individual call.

In any country, locational advantage is the key to success. Today MNCs too need to stay close to their markets. This brings them to countries like India and China. An Indian start-up is no MNC. Further, the people working in a MNC come from widely diverse backgrounds. For some, an urban or corporate culture is all part of daily life. For a large section of our population, it is as alien as the sun rising in the west. A simple matter of hosting a seminar followed by lunch can create a 'flap'. At one of the universities where I was on assignment, we held a major national workshop inviting nationally reputed professors, and senior government bureaucrats, experts in various fields, and some mid-sized industrialists. I had asked the director at the institute about the arrangements for refreshment and lunch. He had dismissed it saying those were such a routine affair that I just need not give it a second thought.

On the day of the programme I found that lunch was being served from large cauldrons – that are used for cooking and usually used in outdoor picnics in India. I was dismayed. Needless to say, the entire place was cluttered and unclean.

Baptism by Fire

The knowledge-driven economy has brought forth a paradigm shift in how the youth looks at an enterprise. Twenty years back and more, one would have set up a manufacturing unit, with the motive of being an ancillary to a large manufacturing facility. The business then was pretty well stacked in favour of corporate. The ancillary (small units) would supply finished and/or semi-finished products to its primary client. The client would make payments over a period of three to six months. The corporate would actually be investing hardly any money in the business. The small units, the ancillary, remained small. This fact had been brought to the notice of the government of the day a number of times.

Except for lip service, nothing was done to see that these units were paid within the stipulated contractual time limit. The system of pricing the ancillary's products was on 'cost' plus a very small processing charge. The ancillary units had to obtain a line of credit from banks. At times, when the payments were further delayed by their clients, the ancillary would borrow from the market at punitive rates of interest. There was no way the ancillaries could stop supplies.

The entire 'cash flow' followed a 'Ponzi' scheme. As I have mentioned the large companies gobbled up all the liquidity. The poor bloke never had any cash reserve to retire gracefully. He had liabilities to the bank, his supplier, and the workers and of course statutory dues[78].

[78] Post liberalisation, many of these large corporate defaulted in payments towards provident funds, ESI, sales tax and other dues. Nothing really happened to the top bosses. The company just closed shop claiming it had no

Statutory dues such as 'sales tax', central excise duties and a myriad of other government liabilities had to be paid on a monthly basis. If they remain unpaid, a penal interest is levied. The money had to be paid within the next calendar month of the invoice/clearance date. The ancillary was supposed to pay cash down for his sales proceeds payments for which he was expected to receive six months down the line.

I have seen so many excellent facilities closing shop. There was no farewell. Nobody knew them outside the closed circle of suppliers and buyers. It always reminds me of a poor swimmer left in mid-Ganges flailing his arms and legs, till the body runs out of steam and he quietly sinks. This analogy may seem pretty grotesque, but that is exactly what has happened to thousands of old-time small industries.

Add to the list of woes the physical efforts needed for all sorts of follow ups. Those were days that did not have emails and fax machines. The telephone worked for hardly six months of the year. The period when the ~~instrument was functional, getting a~~

money. Whereas the owner/s of the ancillary in similar predicament would have his house, bank account attached and also arrested by the local police. The laws have since been made stringent and now large company bosses do get hauled up to prison. But all these years it was Merry Christmas.

connection was a matter of luck. One had to wait for hours to get through a trunk call. A visit to the bank would entail a loss of half a working day at least.

I do salute people and their enterprises that have survived and those who did not, such ordeals and live to tell their tale. Yes, it has been '*baptism by fire*'.

Enjoy the Hurdles – Try and make it Fun time

I have lived in Bombay for some 20 years and more. I found many people from Kolkata and the eastern region that have just landed there without any prior job offers. They knew someone and in some cases not even that. Yet, over the years, through sheer grit and determination they have made their mark. One such group is the musicians that work in the film industry, the main stay of the Bollywood.

The two technology innovations that have changed how the world moves today are the mobile telephone and the internet. Both these technologies were expensive commodities in India as recent as 1995. It was only after 2000 that the usage became a regular feature in our eco-system. Unfortunately, when I had to take the critical decision on my moving shop, both these facilities were not available to me, having business operations in Chennai and Bombay between 1978 and 1984 and 1978 and 1992 respectively, I used to have a major problem in maintaining regular communication.

Today, these are non-issues. Plus the facilities allow very close monitoring, as branch operations need not be manned by very senior staff. The entire process of communications through STD calls, telegrams and courier was expensive, time consuming process and un-dependable. To sum it all, my basic confidence in relocating was lacking. ***There have been many occasion when I rued my inability to take a more decisive step. I used to wonder whether it was a singular failure.*** Anyway, what is done is done.

Years later, to be precise, 24 years later I was approached by a friend and entrepreneur with a similar issue. He was into BPO running a pretty well knit unit in Kolkata. The meltdown in 2007 put him out of the BPO business. He went through the most undesirable process of laying-off his employees. I had been visiting his facilities quite often. I know the pride with which he spoke about his people. As a matter of fact he took me around and introduced me to some of his senior supervisors.

A year or so before he shut down, he had re-modeled the entire space. It really looked classy. He took me around with the pride of a new father showing off his first born. I, too, appreciated the new look and the effort, money and time that went into it.

All good things come to an end. But, the

difference is that in matters like this, it came crashing down. Not only does it shake the foundation of the business confidence, it creates shock waves. I know what those are as I had gone through the same.

He keeps talking to me, asking me whether he ought to relocate. I keep telling him yes, he should. Look, if you want to put in double the effort in rebuilding the enterprise, please identify a place where you would receive twice the gratification. I missed out on that, I do not want him to miss the opportunity.

One thing, I have learnt is that every hiccup, obstacle and failure is an opportunity. As a knowledge startup, with all the contemporary technology at our disposal, one ought to seize the moment. No software can pinpoint the perfect time – *lagna.* It can be done. My contention is it ought to be done using all the resources at our command so as to reach the shores of our Dream.

A pharma company in Kolkata operating here for the past six decades had to close shop in the '70s all of a sudden owing to the political instability in the state. The story goes that the owners travelled to Delhi where they manufactured the same products in a small shed and sold them on the pavements[79] of Delhi. Today, they are one of the leading

[79]I was told by a senior director that the owner and his family members were out there on the street. What Spirit! I salute them.

pharmaceutical companies of the country with sales in thousands of cores of rupees. I am sure they seized the opportunity in building a colossus. That is the spirit.

This society at times behaves strangely. You may have noticed how many a time we just ignore and walk past a person asking for alms. Yet, I find that in the business environment, strangers extending support and words of encouragement. When I had closed down my business, I used to go sit in my office and practically doodle on a piece of paper hoping the paper would come to life and speak to me.

Of course that never happened. However, one day a very senior business man just walked in and asked what I was doing. I said, 'Nothing, I have no business'. He looked at me and said, 'you can't say that, I will give you business whatever you want'. I was taken aback. Here was the guy with whom I had a rocky business relationship which lasted quite a few years.

My belief is that we as people like to see someone fighting. We would like to cheer the fighter and even go to his aid. We probably have an inherent disdain for a loser, especially those that keep whining. It is true some of the poor do starve. It is equally true that a vast numbers that live in hamlet far from cities and equally poor, do not beg. They keep fighting the elements. Some they win. Many a time they lose.

Globalization is a huge challenge. Products

from China keep coming to India sometimes through the official route, that is, after paying customs duty, but often smuggled in. The eastern part of the country has a porous border. These products are cheap and severely undercut our local manufacturers. The time has come to take the bull by its horns. Some Indian entrepreneurs have already contracted Chinese manufacturers for supplies as per specifications. This essentially means the Indian entrepreneurs have financed Chinese manufacturers. For competing in the local market here in India such a strategy is good. But it has taken away our manufacturing industry and local jobs.

14. KNOWLEDGE ENTERPRISE – THE TECHIE

- Baptism by Fire
- The Indian Society largely favors job seekers. It helps in the marriage market

The knowledge economy has been an enabler for the civil society. Examples abound. At this point in time we see around us gizmos like iPhone, Kindle fire and many others.

But the moot question is, whether technology drives the business or does the business need to take cognizance of the need of the civil society. The change in the menu of McDonalds in providing fresh salads and curbing use of *trans fat* stems from the demand by the civil society. Yet, McDonald reached its pinnacle selling items like cheese burgers and Big Mac[80] oozing in trans-fat. Being a smart company it has quickly changed gears.

I find that the bulk of knowledge startups are techies who feel that their technology innovation is the last word in today's world. My statement has come through a bit too strong. On purpose I want to sound as an alarmist as any technology innovation is never a static process. If it was so we will not be using the iPhone today. Suddenly the users of iPhone and the other gizmos find

[80] They continue selling these items.

the gadgets to be so useful that they wonder how they could have survived all these years without them. Funny isn't it? As the renowned film director Ray said in one of his scripts of a film, the public is whimsical. Startup must take stock of the situation – market dynamics.

Soft landing Facilities

How can one plan to setup a facility at a distant place? There is a major obstacle even thinking of doing so, even much before a business plan can be structured. It is called – the comfort zone. Our normal place of residence becomes a comfort zone, with all the spots and blemishes it displays. The first thing that comes to my mind whether we can comfortably relocate? Frankly, there is nothing comfortable about establishing a new facility somewhere else. It is actually the entrepreneur's vision of mid- and long-term locational benefit. Some of the basic tenets are as follows – scout new potential cities and town and try and get the feel whether such a place has the inherent welcome attitude for the outsider. This is very important. An entrepreneur does not have the financial clout to keep changing locations.

Sometime in the late 70s I travelled to the state capital of a neighboring state to meet the MD of the state agency facilitating SMEs. First, the MD walks into his office around noon. I have been waiting for the past hour and a half. The office was empty. There was no one besides me in the waiting room. I was made to wait for another fifteen minutes. When I met him he was curt. After giving a short introduction about my business I asked him what facilities the state government would provide. He asked me to read up the government notifications. His entire attitude was that he could not be bothered. He never thought that he was being paid with tax-payers' money to help people like me. As an entrepreneur, I thought discretion was better than my business plan. If this is how local officials behave when one makes a routine enquiry, what will be the status when I would be neck deep in getting through the government formalities? No, it was surely not a good welcome.

Today one can largely ignore such local officials through the 'soft landing facility' offered by various science parks located in quite a few countries. What does the 'soft landing facility' (SLF) have on offer?

1. The science park offers an office space for two or three days at no cost.
2. It provides information to the company on matters of relevance.
3. It offers lounge facility.
4. A meeting room to interact with local business
5. It facilitates local statutory permissions.
6. For longer period a charge is levied. These charges are lower than market rates, though such facilities are extended only for a fixed period, after which the company is expected to move out.

How does a 'soft landing facility' benefit an entrepreneur?

1. The facility available globally has certain technology-specific focus – pharma, biotechnology, IT, Nano technology, food processing and others. Thus the startups with a bit of research can narrow down to their specific technology SLF.
2. The free-of-charge facility for the first couple of days helps in getting a feel of the place and the local eco-system. This is a great help. Companies can set up meetings as an address is available at that destination.
3. SLFs are extended by those Science Parks and Incubators that have a welcoming attitude for new entrants. This is the crux for the success of an enterprise. An environment of vibrancy and goodwill plays a very crucial part in creating the feel-good factor and the comfort zone.
4. Normally, SLFs provide much needed critical commercial information to the companies well before they physically land at the facility. Thus, by the time a visiting team arrives, they have a well charted program for their activities.

India has few incubators mostly located in academic institutions. Some may have SLF, though I am not aware. But incubations that work within the academic system generally do not encourage startup teams that were never their students. This is not the case with

Science Parks. Science Parks, too, have incubations that extend similar or better facilities than those offered here in India. Of course, we must bear in mind that the incubation program in India gathered steam only after 2000 and there are multiple hiccups and problems that such incubators face. I have already mentioned that some Indian incubators have shown good results with graduating companies. This is their claim. There are no independent audits. However, the numbers are very small to draw any conclusion either way.

15 MIGRATION AND MARKETS

- Keep fighting the odds

All this while, I have been focusing on migrating to greener pastures so as to reap the benefit of a congenial eco-system.

However, let us not forget that our primary aim remains how to access the market, and increase our customer base and thus promote sales.

The new technology arenas of IT (software development and knowledge process) and ITeS (various IT dependent services) have a major advantage over any other businesses. The business is not location specific. In this business, one need not physically be present in order to interact with the customer. Today, many knowledge startups are in IT and ITeS. Surely, this is a boon to such enterprises though certain infrastructure facilities are a must for the company to operate. There is a need for reasonably good rail, road and air services, and at least a few decent hotels. To top it all, there must be a dependable broadband service provider.

Those who are in such business would immediately acknowledge the importance of these facilities.

Making a sweeping statement as I have done in the previous paragraph, must as usual come with a rider.

One of the startup teams had approached me with their business plan that was to be a web portal for home delivery of food from restaurants in cities. To kick off the portal, he needs to carry out a beta testing of the services through the portal. The options are clear. If the team is located in a small town, the number of such eating places would be extremely limited and connectivity of the local population pretty low. It has to be a metro city or a city where the middle class can afford to eat out once in a while. To set up the entire business logistic the team needs to spend considerable time interacting with multiple eating houses, and finalizing the agreements.

For the test marketing, a close follow-up of all feedback needs to be carried out. Once all this is done, the portal need to be tweaked and offered to the general populace. My projection was that the process would take about 18 months after the formal launch to generate revenue. After offering the service in a particular city, the same may be offered at other metros too. There is an advantage. Many food outlets in metros have their outlets or franchise operating in other metros, too.

The Youth need to be Skilled

But startups are not only in IT and ITeS. Today, the knowledge economy has opened up avenues in various types of businesses – skill training, management development programs, event management, hospitality (not only hotels and restaurants, but in various related areas), supply chain management, manpower management in medium and large departmental stores. As of now, in India, most of these businesses need to be located either in a metro or in a large town. The number of people already employed and the potential of future employment in such enterprises far outnumber that of ITeS.

One question that has largely remained unanswered, is why India has suddenly awakened to the need to promote entrepreneurs? I really do not have any definite answer. But my 13 years in establishing technology incubators within academic institutions have given me a small degree of insight. Let me note those in order of importance.

1. All of us, who have gone through the rigors of higher education in the country, intrinsically claim a fair knowledge of education and its standards. Let me qualify this. I am speaking of people who are 35 years and above.
2. The notion of having a fair knowledge of the education system cannot be farther from the truth. Today, students do not

hesitate to question their teachers' abilities. In many academic institutions (especially the private institutions), the young teachers are just marking time. The moment they would get an opening in the government or a corporate, off they go.

3. Barring a few top class institutions, the rest have pay scales that are not only unattractive, they do not encourage the teacher to engage in academic pursuits that could help the institution to gain academic excellence.
4. The government has opened up higher education to private participation; a large section of the youth today enroll in technology education hoping to get a job at the end of the course. It is always the pot of gold at the end of the rainbow.
5. A few years back, principals and other officials of some colleges were assaulted by students who did not get placements after completion of their degree program.
6. The industry added fuel to the fire by claiming that the majority of the technology graduates were unemployable. How sad this is.

Yet, I have no answer to my primary question. Why talk of entrepreneurs? As we all know, only a few students from any college ever seriously plan in venturing on their own. I am sure the government and the civil society groups who speak of entrepreneurship are equally aware of the facts, and at the same time aware that no wishful thinking and financial incentives will create a large group of entrepreneurs. As a matter of fact, wherever financial incentives have been offered, and the funds disbursed, the money has just disappeared.

I believe, at long last, the government in its wisdom decided in imparting skills to people. A new department in the federal government – National Skill Development Corporation (NSDC) – was established to develop various training centers that are not part of an academic institution. Further such training centers must have a business plan to generate revenue to cover their cost and leave a surplus. An initial soft loan is part of such package. And as in any loan that is agreed on, the borrower must show that they have the necessary funds to supplement the loan and organize the program as required.

The basic structure of this program makes eminent sense. Let me analyses this program the way I see it.

1. No one-time grant is given. It is a loan. If the training program is meant to enable people with skills which in turn will make them competent to earn a living, the trainer himself must first practice whatever he is preaching.
2. The money disbursed as grant to various NGOs, academic institutions and similar bodies every year for the past 15/16 years I happen to be aware was money thrown into a bottomless well. If those programs were successful even in parts, this new program would not have been

structured.

3. For all practical purposes, various government departments, as DST, MSME, and NABARD, funded the earlier programs – EDP, EAC, and others –. I had the opportunity to go through the NABARD program. After having conducted more than 70 skill set programs designed by me, I found the NABARD programs faulty and told them so. *They were quite offended.* Nobody dares tell the government funding agency that they are at fault.
4. Further such programs carried out in academic institution are more like a picnic, with a couple of days off from regular lectures and students being provided with tea, snacks and lunch. How better can it be?
5. Fortunately the present program of skill set, by its very stringent financial structure, rules out any fun time and free lunches.

Since participants too need to pay (some from financially deprived community get it absolutely free) I presume they too would be looking for 'value adds'. If such value addition can be achieved, it would create a USP for the training organization.

Thus, there is a method in helping create excellence of the trainers and the training organization. This is a critical necessity.

Since the program is in its nascent stage, I cannot forecast the future[81]. Plus I am given to understand that the department concerned has been approached by a variety of organizations that claim to have excellent faculty of trainers. I realize the difficulty of the parent organization is evaluating such claims as none of these organizations have a track record.

Who are these people that one should target for such training? What will they be trained in?

My interaction with one of the NSDC funded training organizations in Kolkata has brought forth the following.

1. They have focused on candidates that have passed the school certificate exam of class 12 that are held by all Indian states.
2. This particular center has focused on candidates residing in the periphery of Kolkata. Later they would access other small towns.
3. The training is in communication skills. Today, this entails learning to speak English. I am sure they would also teach them to write grammatically correct English that could form the normal business correspondence.
4. Business etiquettes as needed to work in an office or any commercial

[81] The present reckoning of the government is the NSDC has not delivered. I believe there have been some critical drawbacks in the choice of the organizations that were funded.

establishment. This is very important. Most schools have a set of disciplines. But classroom disciplines are dispensed with the moment school is over. It is very common to hear a commotion at any school once the final bell of the school is rung to signify end of a school day.

Etiquette needs to be ingrained. There are occasions when we confuse etiquette with good manners. It is not so. Let me give an example. A customer walks into a shop asking for a refund or a replacement of a product. The particular request cannot be met owing to certain provisions in the sale contract. It is important that the dealing person refuses the request but at same time must maintain etiquette. This etiquette can also be termed as 'professional approach'. The customer may be unhappy at such refusal.

But I believe civility pays. This approach would take time to inculcate in a person. It is a process that needs all round cooperation and a basic urge by the incumbent to learn and practice. Practice, as we all know, makes perfect.

My statements above are definitely not all comprehensive. There are other issues, big and small. I am sure a cohesive effort will show results in a short time.

But there are other areas that need skill training. For long such a need has been glossed over.

Every year scores of students enroll in colleges, good colleges at that, for degree courses in various science subjects. (I am giving this as an example. Non-science subject students too can benefit from the program that I am trying to elaborate on.)

Generally these are physics, chemistry, mathematics and now a variety of life science subjects as botany, zoology, bio-chemistry, biotechnology. Kolkata University has two types of B.Sc. degrees – pass and honors. A reasonably good student generally opts for honors. It would be fair to assume that on an average there would be 500 students in each discipline(the figure of 500 relates to the honors science subjects only; relatively fewer colleges offer such courses owing to lack of lab facilities)[82].

On completion of the B.Sc. degree course, most students want to pursue the post graduate program. But the number of seats in PG is limited. Some then opt for courses that they feel are job-oriented – IT skills, MBA program etc. Some do not try this route and take up a job of a school teacher or a private tutor. A teacher's job or making ends meet through private tuitions are both unviable at the entry level.

My point is that all these students are above

[82] All colleges that offer the honors course do not necessarily have adequate lab facilities.

average. It is owing to their superior performance in school-leaving exams, they could gain admission to the honors program. It will be a shame if a Botany Student lands a BPO or call center job[83].

In a country like India with diverse groups of people and a variety of social norms, any one program with a rigid structure is never going to work. If we do see a homogeneous group, it will be in metro cities. This group is very small compared to the rest of the population in the country.

I was watching one of the shows on television where this lady of Indian origin from Punjab and now a naturalized citizen of the US, a neural scientist by profession, wanted to become a chef. It was her dream from childhood. Her mother was horrified, "Do you want to become a servant?" It makes not an iota of difference that her parents too have been living in the US for the past 25 years and more, where dignity of labor is not in words but in deeds.

When I told my family in the early '70s that instead of becoming a civil servant I would like to set up my own enterprise, the immediate response was that businessmen *are crooks*. Sure some are, but we cannot paint everyone with the same brush.

Before we try to impart skills to say a class 10

[83] We keep stating that both in schools and colleges there is a dearth qualified teachers. It is a shame.

dropout in a location where caste plays a predominant role, one must gauge what sort of skill training would make the person eligible for a livelihood.

I am convinced that the areas of imparting skills be rigorously followed with due safe guards. We should not have adverse publicity as did happen to the critical area of 'family planning' during the days of 'Emergency'.

The safe areas to my mind are the skill set training for qualified graduates. It is a fact that every Indian wants 'white collar' jobs and not 'blue collar' jobs but at some point of time both will overlap and one will not be able to distinguish. I met a Russian in the US who is a furniture salesman. Earlier in Russia he was a professor of mathematics at Moscow University. He was very pleasant to talk to. And he is very happy to be in the US.

A leading global company manufacturing road laying equipment has an army of support service engineers. All these personnel come from engineering colleges with degrees in electrical, mechanical, computer and electronics engineering. They are entrusted with attending to customers wherever located normally in the middle of nowhere, and attend to equipment that is malfunctioning. Earlier on it used to be a mechanic's job. Well these people are today's mechanics.

Probably the family is impressed as the

incumbent is provided with a vehicle, a mobile phone and a flashy designation. Owning a car in India, even today, is a status symbol. A janitor in the US rides a vehicle which at times would be a shade pricey. But, here the eco-system differs. And we must take cognizance of the fact.

But one must accept that on-the-job experience as a support technical team does wonders for the individual. From being trained as a techie in the college, he now learns to work on his PR skills, have an attitude of 'never say die' as the guys in the road laying business are on a tight schedule and any breakdown causes a high level of stress, and tempers are frayed. People who work in the support team say that these customers do not tolerate fools.

Well, that can be pretty stressful. Further the technician is supposed to mail a report on the breakdown to his principal, from the work site. No excuses. The Indian climate of hot and hotter, wet and wetter is definitely not a shade close to the svelte depiction of executives we see in the print and electronic media. Unfortunately, students in colleges are ignorant of the *'dark side of the moon'*.

Skill set training need to create an impact so as to help create a means of livelihood for the vast majority of unemployed and under employed. Industry has time and again been vocal on poor quality of graduates. I know that they have specified technology pass out. But the largest section of the youth study for basic degree programs generally in liberal arts. What will happen to this group? As far as livelihood is concerned, there is need for equal opportunity.

Just a few days ago I had ordered a book on short stories by W. Somerset Maugham. Since there were some hitches, I called up to enquire. The person on the other end could hardly pronounce the author's name. After some prompting from my end he could barely pronounce - Somerset but not 'Maugham'. After I finished with my query I helped him pronounce 'Maugham' as 'MoM'. I am sure we would expect the salesman of a leading bookstore to be familiar with names of authors. I cannot blame the chap. The store is lacking in its training.

16 FUN TIME

- Dream

Entrepreneurship is not always serious stuff. It is fun. As an entrepreneur, it is for us to view our life the way we would like it to be. How can entrepreneurship and establishing an enterprise not be fun? After all, we as entrepreneurs have decided that our lives need some meaningful goals.

Is it not fun to be the master of your daily work schedule? That one need not hurry to work because the boss is out there breathing down one's neck.

Is it not fun, when a customer comes to you and compliments you on your product or service?

I remember a couple of persons walked up to me 10 years after I had closed down my tape recorder manufacturing unit, saying that their equipment still works. I was a quite surprised and asked them whether they had to get it serviced in the intervening period. They replied in the negative. I personally would never imagine that a piece of hardware that sold at Rs.500/- would be going strong even after 15 years. But surely to me it was real fun. Boy that sounds good!

Blood, sweat and tears, yes, but after that it is joy and fun. And I would urge all entrepreneurs to take up this challenge as a fun activity. It will work. People like those with a positive cheerful look. Even if a customer walks in with a complaint, he will definitely walk out with a much better frame of mind. You are the fun guy. As a fun guy you also understand if your customer is unhappy. And you will do everything to make him happy. And this happiness is contagious.

An entrepreneur essentially charts his own path. That by itself is the fun part. As I have mentioned in previous chapters, entrepreneurship is not a 21st century invention. Probably, we can state that it is a discovery by the knowledge groups. The knowledge driven entrepreneurship has brought forth a new business model in the civil society. I had already mentioned about the revolution in communication by mobile telephony.

Entrepreneurship has caught the imagination of the civil society. I believe that the civil society has far greater faith in the benevolence of technology than what it had in the past, with large corporations involved in most products and services. Well, large corporation do exist even today. But people as Bill Gates and Steve Jobs have definitely shown the world that enterprises that started in garages a couple of decades ago, surpass the large companies in their market capitalization. And this is a miracle. None of those companies in their growth stage went out and carried a massive media blitz, or had employed hot shot grads from leading US schools. It was simply because they did not have the sort of resources.

Instead, they built their capital with their intellectual property – their own minds. The last two decades have also seen the growth in importance of intellectual property and intellectual property rights. IP is a commodity that is traded.

Why is civil society an inherent part of the entrepreneurship endorser?

I think that our enterprise can succeed if it can identify a niche clientele. It need not be overly dependent on civil society. For example, hi-fashion products have very limited and niche client. Some of them are doing exceedingly well in terms of revenue generation as compared to software, hardware and hospitality, for example.

But, if you compare with a product line like Levi's jeans, or Nike shoes and similar clothing and accessories brands, their global sales and multipoint sales are far greater than those in hi-fashion. Obviously their visibility is also higher. It goes without saying the word Levi's connotes a pair of Jeans. It is similar to the word Xerox which incidentally is a copyright logo of the Xerox Corporation. With many photocopying products flooding the market, the word Xerox has taken on the generic name, even though the equipment is not from the Xerox Corporation.

Xerox through technological innovation had invented a device for the civil society which is not only useful; the civil society has come forth and endorsed the need.

Job and the Society

In some of the developing economies like India, a person holding a job has higher social status.

Before liberalization and the advent of the IT sector as a major destination for the qualified youth, everyone angled for a government job. In addition, the divisive effects of the Indian caste system, such jobs as those of the Indian Administrative Services, the provincial civil services and the other categories of government jobs have helped create a new class in the society.

IT, financial and hospitality sectors and a few others like the event management have created a new class of employees. These fortunately are a very homogenous group, who as far as I know, do not carry the old baggage.

It is extremely refreshing in interacting with this new breed of youngster. Growing up in a family where most members were in government jobs gave me enough insights into the machination of the system, the constant bickering, the all ominous political interference are things I was not looking for in my career. I think few in the IT crowd ever think of joining government service.

The society places a high level of importance to the networked marriage. All I can say, each to his own. In India, families prefer to have the daughter-in-law to be just a housewife. A working girl is a strict no no. There are innumerable instances where the girl is dissuaded from pursuing an academic program. A girl having a higher qualification than the boy does not find favor in marriages. Yes, we still have a long way to go. I can only hope that the Indian society would one day reach there.

Surely news headline of the member of the Indian Foreign Service bashing his wife does not do us credit. I strongly believe that the civil service examination ought to include a psychological profiling of the candidate. Our rulers must be seen as people who have an attitude of extending a helping hand towards the general population that they are supposed to deal with. A high IQ taciturn person cannot fit the profile of an efficient administrator.

At the time I graduated in Physics (Hons.) from Kolkata University, quite a few of my friends had applied to the IIM, Kolkata. We had no clue as to what this program was. All we knew was that it can get us some very good jobs in leading corporate houses. Of course at that point such corporate houses were few. There is no point in mentioning their names, as they have all disappeared barring a couple. However, I did know from my dad's network that corporate houses employed only those guys whose parents were some influential big shot. Oh, I forgot to mention, this was for the managerial positions. The other positions, that are non-managerial, were worse than government clerical jobs.

The piece of cake for a MBA grad is the successful placement in an investment bank. Investment banks pay very well. Probably it owes to surfeit of money that gullible people like us give them. If things go well, there is a lot of crowing, otherwise there are stories that abound in Wall Street after the market meltdown is 2007. The best part is, nobody is actually held responsible, and there is no question of the money that people have invested to be redeemed. I wonder which other business gives such wonderful returns?

Lee Iacocca in his book Iaccoca An Autobiography– (Lee Iaccoca and William Novak 1984) ridiculed the Wall Street guys. Nobody paid any attention. You may say that well there was a period when investors did make money. It is just too bad that now people have lost all. A logic that could well mean, that it has evened out the gains with the losses. Why do we say that a Ponzi scheme is illegal? A guy like Madoff is locked up for the next 150 years.

It has traditionally been a system of give and take. In ancient times it was barter. Even a few decades ago, people in certain regions of the world used the barter system for trade. There was no concept of a currency guaranteed by the state as the concept of the state was very vague.

Just as in barter either party took a conscious decision on a trade by looking at the merchandise on offer, in today's world the buyer-customer can be short-changed – the commodity on sale is usually a piece of paper detailing a lot of promises.

The investment banks and the finance companies rely on their masterly arbiters in selling dream packages –sub-prime bonds. And they have been eminently successful in selling some worthless paper and raking in huge amounts of money that they in turn have invested in personal assets. Companies like Lehman Brothers, went down the tube, but the managers flourished. These guys were smart enough not to invest in the same worthless papers.

17 SOCIAL ENTREPRENEURSHIP

Yes, it is an eye opener, and a very painful one at that. People at large are speaking of inclusive growth, whereby the benefits of the economy can reach the poorest of the poor. As C. K. Prahlad in his book has mentioned, there is money to be made even at the 'Bottom of the Pyramid'.

The knowledge startups are concentrating more and more in social entrepreneurship. As mentioned earlier, a business must be able to cater to the demand of the user who is the buyer. Only then it will be sustainable.

There are innumerable lessons to be learnt from multitude of small business across our country. In India, having a cup of tea is a major pastime. We do not drink beer as is done in some western countries. There are innumerable small tea shops, the majority on the pavements, some just a hole in the wall, a few ramshackle shacks. These outlets open their business as early as 6 in the morning and continue till 10 in the evening, a few even later. Majority of these sell just tea and some biscuits. That's their basic merchandise.

A large number have committed clients. The price of a cup of tea in a particular city is more or less the same. The tea is freshly brewed and served piping hot. There is usually a bench or a few stools where one can sit. The shopkeeper never tries to hustle the person drinking his tea. He gladly serves a cuppa and waits for his money after the person finishes his cup. Rarely does a customer walk away without paying. I have found that the tea served in a particular tea stall, has the same flavor day in and day out. That and the attitude of the stall owner is the USP. Customer Friendly, Quality, Price.

The knowledge enterprise at times gets heady with the Innovation of the product or service. Little thought is given to the three issues as mentioned above.

This is similar to the advance booking now available for people who plan to travel to outer space sometime in future. It will cost a bomb, but there are a number of rich people who have shown their inclination. The question is, whether this will be sustainable business. If so, surely at a much reduced price as we have seen in case of mobile telephone services.

In India pre-2000, the mobile telephone subscription was prohibitive. The number of subscriber base obviously was low. The service providers approached the government for financial support. Shortly thereafter, as the call rates were pruned, the number of subscribers shot up.

I remember having subscribed to a mobile service in 1996. A single call was Rs.15/- (if I remember correctly). We were also charged for incoming call. Today a single call is rarely above Re. 1/-. Incoming calls and SMS are free. Subscribers of mobiles phone have seen double digit growth for the past few years. Service providers, as I understand, have recovered their investment many times over.

Of course, the strategy will change depending on the nature of business. Every business cannot aspire for double digit growth year after year. Again a very capital intensive business cannot expect to recover their investments within a short time without critically crippling the enterprise.

A story that made the rounds in Kolkata some years back was about a business man who bought a tea garden in Dooars, West Bengal. The states of West Bengal and Assam have extensive tea plantations. Of course Darjeeling Tea (Darjeeling is in West Bengal) is world famous.

Tea output is cyclical. The yield of tea peaks in cyclical pattern and even the tea prices that depend on auction house prices, peak in cyclical order.

After buying the tea garden the businessman found that though tea shrub is a perennial plant, it requires to be tended day in and day out leading to substantial expense. He waited for the price to peak. Once it did touch the peak, he plucked all the leaves of the tree, sold the same and earned handsome returns, uprooted the bare tree and sold these as firewood, subsequently he sold the land too, to a developer of resort.

In all probability the story is concocted. But it is true that smaller gardens were bought by local businessmen from the planters and quite a few have been turned into housing complex.

When we speak of business in the context of the knowledge domain, one point does arise – is the focus going to be on making money and lots of money?

It surely goes without saying that there ought to be enough money to keep the establishment on its feet. The paradox is whether we follow the method of stripping a running business? Or we make an effort in sustaining and growing the business?

This question is not easy to answer. In the Indian context, many businesses have grown in leaps and bounds by such practice of stripping. There is a major legal dispute being adjudicated at the Kolkata High Court right now[84] (Feb 13). Money is a huge magnet. Principle and ethics happen to take a much lower order of precedence. Moneyed people are respected in our society. Not only in Indian context, world over these are the influential people. Here in India, a poor person is always in awe of the rich.

We see such business people getting round tricky issues with ease. We all see that they are invited to all the important platforms one can think of. We see their wards in fancy cars mowing down pedestrians, and then being let off with a minor slap on the wrist.

The environment around us surely is a major influence. Knowledge enterprises in India received a fillip with such stories of a handful of committed entrepreneurs who were faceless people for decade and more. Nobody knew them or even wanted to know. Once the going became profitable, everyone got going. That is the beauty of the human nature. Everyone wants to buzz around the queen bee.

[84] The matter of Dunlop and its owner Mr. Ruia. The government and the erstwhile employees are the litigants against the present owners.

Dream

It is people with dream. They create knowledge enterprises. It is their singular dream to achieve and their vision in achieving the goals that make them a success. I do not think the glitter of wealth normally cloud their judgment as can be seen with other business people. When one reads about Madoff's lifestyle, the cost of a single dinner, his cigar and other trappings, one cannot help in thinking that his goal was to ride the ritzy environment of society, and somewhere he lost his way, and landed in jail. To me the fact that his son committed suicide after he was incarcerated is terribly sad and surely not worth all the wealth that Madoff had acquired.

The present buzz about entrepreneurship, the frequent pronouncements from various business platforms, the high powered groups pontificating on critical issues, make me conclude that the beat of the drums have drowned the voice.

I was invited to a premier program where selected entrepreneurs were to be felicitated. One of them was a team that I had mentored. During a break, a correspondent of a national daily while speaking to me realized I was the mentor of the winning team. The lady wanted to speak to the entrepreneur. I pointed to him.

After sometime the entrepreneur came over requesting me to join the discussion. It was not a discussion. It was a press interview. The correspondent was asking structured questions which would have been appropriate for a corporate. Questions like how many employees in which department and other related matters that are part of a corporate structure.

A startup team of three to four persons do not have a company with departments. Neither do they have a HR manager. They cannot afford a marketing manager, or a yearly publicity budget. Many of these matters, though important, are played by the ear. Revenue is generated by tagging on to one medium or large client who is serviced by the team members.

My startup team member was at a loss for words. He had no clue how to respond to the question of the correspondent, as to who are the target customers. Have they carried out a market survey? If so what is the sample size? What are their sales projections? Have they calculated the fund requirements and source of funding so as to achieve such targets?

Surely extremely pertinent questions[85].But,

---

[85] In my early days as an entrepreneur, I used to represent a leading German company manufacturing Stamping Foils. Once while visiting a leading MNC with the German representative of the company, we were lead to the storehouse by an executive, who then

how can a startup who is wobbly find all the answers? If you notice most of such interviews is a short paragraph in the print media. The media wants news, news that would be of interest to its readers. Without such inputs there is no news. Of course a startup would like to be covered by a leading print media. It helps create certain credibility at very little cost. However, this credibility should not be confused with brand building. At most, it works as an introduction to the business world. At least, the startup has something going for its confidence building. Not bad. But the entire exercise is transient.

One can extrapolate this to groups that do not participate in such exercises and remain absolutely unknown. They work within their own networks and the inherent strength of their network helps them to forge ahead. Let me be very candid. Whatever publicity there could be, the network is essential for sustenance of any startup. No association of business and industry ever make an effort to reach out. I am not looking at 'lip-service'. Network members are far closer to ground

---

proceeded to list out his complaints. In between the executive stopped and stepped out. The German chap turned to me and said that all large companies have surplus staff that creates issues where there are none. I was quite shocked. Whatever the executive of the MNC was pointing out were ridiculous to say the least. In the past two decades the company I had visited had closed down. So much for such high sounding stuff.

realities than bureaucrats and top corporate honchos who are primarily interested in 'lobbying' and enhancing their own perks. My question is who would lobby for these bright young startups? And it is an accepted fact that entrepreneurs create wealth for the nation. Some in the civil society do reach out. These are from the silent majority that has kept the legacy of self-employment alive everywhere. A microscopic section is from industry. Most of such people are professionals who do come forth on their own. Yes this is what keeps this movement going.

18 LIFE IS NOT FAIR

-People in Business we look up to, did rough it out.
-There is no reason why we should not.
-As Bill Gates has said, 'Life is not Fair'.

Many a times startups crib about various issues that dog them in their business. As Bill Gates says 'Life is not fair'. The earlier one accepts reality; it is so much easier.

I conducted a workshop at IIT Bombay named 'Marketing Mantra'[86]. But believe me, there is no 'mantra' for business. The only two things I would stress on are – passion and determination.

Once the enterprise starts generating revenue, the startups latch on to network of traders, actual users and of course government revenue officials. The network has a lot of 'static'[87] that at times drown the

[86] Mantra is a Hindi word for religious chants. The word is loosely used to denote some sort of alchemy.

efforts in operating as per the plan. And this 'static' is 24X7.

What sort of advice do you keep receiving?

Do not raise the bill now. You can save 'x' amount of tax and interest, that you need not make a bill for the entire amount and collect the balance amount in cash. And those of you who are in business can add to this list.

Business must generate revenue. And obviously the revenue ought to be in excess of the expenditure so as to keep the company afloat. Further, not only should the revenue be in the plus, but it must also be enough for the company to build up its capital – corpus. This money will help the enterprise in developing its business program as it goes along.

Now the question that arises is how much is enough? In my business I realized in a period of three years that I must generate enough funds to rent an office space, a storage facility and a space to repair the equipment I sell. Till such time I was operating from my residence. From a situation where I had no employee in year one, after I rented the premise I employed seven people by year two. Well that was quite a load. I used to worry about money every month just before the salary payment date. In the past 40 years I

---

[87]Static as in wireless communication – radio frequency interference.

have always paid the salary on the seventh of every month without fail.

Like any youngster at 26, I used to wonder how people in business made the pot of gold that I keep hearing. Quite a few owners of leading Indian corporations have their residence in Kolkata[88]. I used to wonder as to whether I would be able to generate the sort of wealth these people have made for themselves. As I progressed in my venture my network was abuzz with stories of various 'deals' these people entered into, which of course gave them a fabulous windfall. By the way there were some investigations and sometime court cases. In the end, everything was hunky-dory.

Actually we forget such matters in nearly a twinkling of the eye. There were temptations in trying out some of what my associates claimed were innocuous deals. By such time I was pretty astute. I could quickly find out the areas that could land me in some sort of muddle. My associates would laugh at my hesitations. To each her own. But the long and short is, *I did not find the pot of gold.* However, my business survives till the present. Sixty percent and more of the owners of business in my network are today twiddling their thumbs after they were forced to close shop. Do they have their pot of gold? I don't know. I can only wish them well.

---

[88] In the 50s & 60s Kolkata used to be the business capital. Today it is Mumbai. Kolkata has slipped way down.

The common refrain I keep hearing even today, you got to do, what everyone is doing here in India. At least a couple of decades back it was not so much about executives in corporates and just a handful of bureaucrats. Now, it is an altogether different ballgame[89]. As I mentioned earlier in the book, quite a few mid-sized businesses folded up owing to various government prosecutions. A few of the owners were incarcerated. I call them the unlucky ones as the majority could elude such stringent prosecution. The scale of such corruption is mind boggling. I wonder why such deterrent actions of the early years did not have the intended effect. Instead the size has swelled up to gigantic proportions. Why?

[89] The print media reported a few days back that a lowly employee at the check post of a state had amassed an astounding amount of money running into crores. Obviously he could not have been operating in the manner he had operated without the connivance of some senior official. And there are such incidents reported nearly every day.

5 ADAPTABILITY

- Entrepreneurial Advantages for people from Business families.
- Learn from experiences of other business
- There is no alternate to change
- Business is run by Acumen
- Innovative continuously

Time to Change Track

Beyond all that I have mentioned in the pages I have written on areas of concern, I do realize that a startup in a business family is "conditioned" in. Before the entrepreneur from a business family starts his venture, he has already made a detailed study of the market, the technology and most critically, the source of fund.

How does he do it?

In earlier times, I have never seen a detailed project report (DPR) been written by a startup, except for an awful project report

(PR) that everybody put together to submit to the bankers for a loan. The content of such a PR was always a figment of imagination.

Let me narrate an incident. By the end of the '80s, the electronics trade –consumer electronics, TVs, radios, music systems– was declining. A business group from Kolkata that I happened to know requested my advice in establishing a cement plant in Odisha. I knew nothing of cement or the potential of the market. Internet was not a tool available.

I was intrigued and asked the owner why he was considering investing in the cement trade? He countere by asking why I went into health care. It so transpired that his family members, each of whom were in independent business, did multiple brain storming sessions. They all realized that retail and distribution of consumer durables were in the decline. They unanimously agreed that one just has to shut shop and get out of the business.

But then do what? The earnings of the business primarily go into running the household. A part of that earning is the corpus. For a medium level business house launching an IPO is/ was not a very prudent decision. It is true that during the first stock market boom, best known as Harshad Mehta period, many fly by night operators floated companies and launched IPOs. Later some managed to flee, that is disappear[90]. A few unlucky ones[91] went to prison. Harshad Mehta died a few years later. No one is wiser to what did happen.

Let me come back to my friend's idea of a mini cement plant in the state of Odisha. He narrated that once, while travelling by train to Gujarat from Kolkata, he met a co-passenger who was in the process of setting up a similar industry. Since the train journey was for two and a half days, my friend questioned his fellow passenger in detail and found that the raw materials are available in abundance in Odisha, a neighboring state of West Bengal.

Once he came back to Kolkata, he went to Odisha to do a recce and stayed at various places for nearly a month and collected all necessary data on market, raw material sourcing, skilled labor, local laws etc.

At the same time he purchased a few books on cement manufacturing technology that is essential for establishing a cement plant and also collected the names and addresses of capital equipment manufactures.

He got back to his family members and asked them to find the market mechanics that

[90]They could disappear as the initial company details provided were fictitious. Till 1992, the Department of Company Affairs of the government was largely lax and corrupt.

[91] The Indian business community calls such people fools.

govern cement market. How is it sold? Through a distributor, or directly to large customers? How big is the retail trade in the city? How many players are there besides the biggies? How do smaller players work the market?

The entire exercise took a year. It took my breath away. Here was this guy who knew nothing about an industry (none in the family is an engineer), but within a year had gathered enough knowledge to make a foray into the industry.

I was requested to look into their financial projections for capital and working funds as loans from bank. I remember telling him that working capital would be difficult to come by. His capital requirement with respect to the entire financial needs was low. If he went to a bank, the entire company has to be hypothecated. They heard me out. Another year went by before we met. I asked him about his company. He explained that after considering my views on the bank loan, his family members had decided not to go to a bank. The family financed the entire business. And they had already started production!

Be Prepared to Learn

In 1987, I decided to shift gears, re-located to Kolkata and established a health care establishment at Gariahat, a shopping district of the city. Over next few years, I toyed with the idea of opening a nursing home and/or a diagnostic facility. I gave up both the ideas and stuck to a polyclinic[92] where senior medical specialists provide consultation.

By 1990, Pearl Clinic had earned a respectable image. Unfortunately, the same could not be said of my income from the clinic. I resisted all ideas of tweaking the medical domain to earn more. In hindsight, I am grateful to the Lord for my will power.

However, I soon realized that we ought to run a specialized center on our own. I planned that the medical service so offered will be totally under our management. In a polyclinic, the attending doctors are fully in control. We have no say whatsoever in their nature of practice or consultation charges. I saw that doctors within a span of five years increased their consultation charges by 400%, from Rs.90/- in 1990 to Rs.400/- in 1995.Phenomenal! Yet, they would be reluctant in increasing the service charges to the center. However, I must admit that, at all times, extremely cordial relations were maintained.

I was planning to open another health care facility. At the same time, I was reluctant in having a similar setup. For two years. I sat on the idea. One day, I thought to myself why is it that there are no medical center that advices people on aesthetics. Beauty parlors abound but poorly trained people man most

[92]Doctors' chamber with more than one medical practitioner available for consultations.

of those. At least that was the situation in the mid-'90s in Kolkata.

Unfortunately, I had no technical competence on how to go about with my new idea. I spoke to a few dermatologists in Kolkata, and then, suddenly, out of the blue, I met one who gave me a two-hour briefing on cosmetology. It was a road map that suited me to the "T". I decided to meet the Queen of Aesthetics, Shahnaz Hussain. My meeting at her center in Delhi is an interesting narration, which I shall leave for later. She was most helpful and she also detailed a road map for the center over a span of three hours. This discussion set the ball rolling and in the next six months, I opened my center with the help of my wife Minakshi, who is a qualified medical practitioner. Today, I am happy to note that the center is run exclusively by us. And we have no dearth of clients.

All that I have mentioned earlier about marketing, I put it in-practice at this center. As days went by, corporate houses have entered the market. They have huge marketing budgets. Skin care products bring in massive revenues[93] for these companies. It is also interesting to note that, whereas traditional cosmetic companies have upgraded their products, leading drug manufacturers have also come into the fray

[93] Fair and Lovely is sold as a whitening cream by the thousands, just to name one such brand.

with highly trained product representatives.

I had a vision of a new approach to health care. I kept at it for two years not losing sight of my ultimate aim even for a moment. And I succeeded. In 1995, when I established this center, did I know that the market would evolve so rapidly? Absolutely not. Actually we could generate surplus revenue only by end of 1997. But the inputs I had gathered from very dependable sources way back in 1993-94 were absolute nuggets. I could sift through the huge mass of market data to hit 'pay dirt'. This is one of the ways to work the 'knowledge domain'.

It is my view that knowledge domain is not only about state-of-the-art technology. It is primarily how we use our intellect in charting a road map to success in our chosen field. Technology is an essential enabler. But business is run by acumen. One of the biggest challenges for me in mentoring startups is their innate love to speak about their technology. It always takes some time to make them see the entire picture.

Innovate Continuously

A few months after I had assumed the responsibility of establishing an Entrepreneurship Development Cell (EDC) supported by DST, Government of India, at St. Xavier's College, I was approached by a startup team. The leader of the team was a technologist who had qualified in computer sciences from a university overseas. He had set up a team of four along with another techie, one finance guy and one marketing chap. A year or may be two earlier he had successfully accessed government seed money to the tune of Rs.13 lacs.

By the time he had come to discuss his business with me he had no money left in the kitty. I asked him as to what he expected from me.

This team wanted me to give them some advice in getting funds. Before I went into the issues raised, I asked the team leader to brief me on the company and its set-up.

The team leader spent an inordinately long time in explaining the technicalities of his product. He tried to do a sort of SWOT. I nudged him to the other areas of finance and marketing.

I was surprised when he told me that the finance guy will brief me on that. The finance guy really had nothing to say. All he said was that the product team would ask for money and he would approve.

Then it was the turn of the marketing chap. He went into a long winded narration that had no substance. Ultimately, I could pin him down to the fact that there were no customers and there was no awareness in the market of the product. However, he insisted that quite a few seminars and workshops had been held to create awareness.

But where is the revenue? Who is ready to pay for the services that the company is providing?

This is a typical example of technology startups. Even though the team comprises of qualified persons, they somehow fail to get the feel of the market and lose sight of the goal..

I always advise startups to work backwards - the market, the logistics, the product/ services. If this route is followed, I am sure they would never lose sight of the actual end user –the *end user.*

A startup I had been mentoring developed a gas leak detection device. By the time I came in contact, they already had a fairly decent exposure in the local media. Being graduate engineers from the local college helped and the media highlighted their achievement. I am sure they too must have been elated.

Unfortunately, they were finding it difficult in identifying customers. Obviously revenue generation was poor. Administrative costs were mounting. They were in discussion with a few major companies. But the final decision on a major contract takes an inordinately long time. And time was not in their favor. They needed funds to run the show. They needed funds to produce the equipment. It was a chicken-and-egg story. Even if they did receive a contract, they had no money to fulfill the contract.

We discussed the main issues, most

importantly, how to get some money, immediately.

- From some government schemes
- As advance from the customer
- From banks

After some brainstorming, we decided that funding from bank would be the most viable approach. But banks would need a signed contract from a Class I company. We got stuck. Apparently, there was no resolution of the issues.

I suggested they relook at the marketing strategy. Who could be the customers? Believe me, they could not think of any except these major buyers (govt. oil companies) and the domestic consumers. Therefore, the questions that remained were:How to sell to individual customers? They really had no clue. They spoke of advertisement in the media, hand bills etc. But all these cost a fair packet.

How to sell to the major companies?

I then asked them to take a look at the product. Can this product not be tweaked into a gas and fire alarm system? Very easily, they said. How long will that tweaking take? A few days. Good. Tweak the product.

How can we now build confidence leads in our customers and who would those customers be. In an order of priority we tried to identify them.

The big companies that store and sell LPG in bulk. This is first in the list as they had already entered into a negotiation over a period of six months.

- Small and medium eating houses (restaurants and small eateries).
- Canteens in educational institutions and companies
- Kitchens of student hostels
- Kitchens of star hotels in the city.

Since we knew some of the owners of these hotels, we approached them and installed these gadgets free of charge in their kitchens. Our request was that we shall be collecting data from time to time and they too would provide us a feedback. Though the product was ready for quite some time, it was never put in a field test. It just never occurred to the team that the product required such testing. Such an approach helped us in further modifying the product once we analyzed the data received from the various locations.

From a marketing perspective, we could share such results with our prospective clients. Since the hotels were premier ones, the clients too could verify the same.

This team participated in the MIT Emtech 2011 challenge and won the award for the Best Social Entrepreneur of the year. It helped the company in getting a national coverage. The team members received a major fillip to their confidence levels and quite a few enquiries and orders for the product.

What was it that made it possible for the company to achieve what it set to do just in a period of six months? A clear picture of the market and the critical feedback from the end-user that helped them to tweak the product.

20 EXPECT THE UNEXPECTED

Let me share my experience. I used to manufacture small portable tape recorders (1983-88), the one you will find people carry for picnics or during a short outing. It was a mains and battery set. It was priced very reasonably to be within the purchasing limits of students. Mid-80s small scale manufacturers were not Brand savvy. All that was needed a name of the product. Some of the products in the market had names such as, hold your breath – Shalimar, Toofani. Mine was a sedate Pentax 100[94]. What was more important was the model number. I stopped manufacturing these after 1988, as there were a large number of similarly priced imported sets in the gray market. The finish of those products was far better. I thought it would be prudent to exit.

I continued to receive enquires for the product till 1995/96. The last unit that came to me for repairs was in 1998, 11 years after I had wound up. I remember customers coming up and asking me the reasons for not producing the sets and that they liked the tonal quality, I could only thank them. There

[94] The prized compliment was from my sales tax consultant who was also the consultant to Shalimar the highest selling brand. He will from time to time buy my product as gifts. When asked why not Shalimar, his refrain was I don't want my friend to bad mouth me. I wonder how Shalimar sales were far higher than mine.

were times when I did toy with the idea of restarting. However, prudence as a businessman held me back, as after liberalization the Indian industrial scene had undergone a radical change[95]. By then big Indian brands have disappeared from the market.

When I started my medical center in Kolkata way back in 1987, I had already decided that I would like to do something for the people of the particular locality in Kolkata. I had not planned it for a growth path, more like a decent place with top class medical consultant in various disciplines of healthcare. I was very choosy and thus for the first two years my business lost money with hardly a couple of doctors. But I did achieve my goal of having top class consultants; I did not want to add diagnostic facilities or minor surgeries. There are quite a few small nursing homes[96] near mine and the same is the case with diagnostic labs. My friends told me that the *moolah* was in the latter two. It is true, but there were other issues involved in running a business in the

[95] One major change has been the phenomenal growth of the IT service sector. Some critics say that these are body shop. But one thing is indisputable. There is money to be made in the sector. Smart businessmen shunned the rigmarole of manufacturing, in some cases shut down the facility and joined the IT gravy train.

[96] Small hospitals

latter two.

As with the type of center I run it is a polyclinic, doctors after few years tend to leave for various reasons. Once they leave there is a vacuum. One day a patient approached me at the clinic. He asked me why we do not have a neurologist. I told him, no neurologist has ever shown any inclination to set up his chamber here. He looked at me and said with a tone of finality that if we really wanted one, with our reputation we will surely have one. And since all our doctors were very reputed, the same would be the case with the new entrant. I was stupefied. How could he come to such conclusion? He said, you have quite a name and the *trust* of the people. Well, that is what a Brand does for you.

When I started in 1972, I used to be a distributor. My principal was COSMIC STEREO. It was a small medium enterprise, what we term as SSI. The consumer Electronics Industries had many small, medium and micro enterprises. But there were at least three large powerful companies. People like us, small enterprises were generally involved in selling their product close to the place of their operations. Cosmic on the other hand tried its hand at the national market through the distributors.

Such a strategy had a very limited benefit. First and foremost the entire logistic to reach the various distributors needed to be structured. States' Tax laws were a big hindrance. Road transportation was the only means as air freight charges were prohibitive. Goods transported by road reached the destinations with various degrees of physical damages[97].

The large companies had dedicated transporter that shipped door to door. The companies had their own depot at all major cities. Our retail outlets were reluctant to handle our product lines. Our sales support services were below par.

I realized after about a year, I was a green horn, that something needs to be done quickly otherwise with hardly any sales I would earn a pittance and ultimately my business would fold up.

Thus I quickly set up a reasonable good after sales service employing a person who would visit the retail outlets, collect the material and deliver the same after it has been serviced. I was busy throughout the day with business matters. At night I used to repair the defective equipments. In a short span not only did my sales volume grow, the shop owners realizing my competence would ask for my advice on products of my competitions. It was my USP that has remained with me, and though I was the newest entrant in the distribution network, I clocked the highest sales outside the home

[97] The highway were not properly maintained which lead to a large number of accidents and damages to the goods.

territory – Mumbai. This lead I could keep for the next 12 years.

Once I could achieve this goal, various opportunities and business proposals came my way. At times it was a bit unnerving as my sales grew exponentially; I found it difficult to manage the various lines of business. My mentor Mr. Manubhai Desai was always at hand to guide me. The other surprising point was that none of the business houses that approached me asked for any upfront payments. I used to wonder why.

Much later I realized that business anywhere needs a doorway to the markets. No sensible business house is really interested in a one-time deal unless the guy is a crook. The supplier has an establishment with a monthly expense account. He needs to plan his finances accordingly. Thus we all look for people who could access market and are in a position to give relevant feedback so that the principal can take corrective measures and plan his production.

One of companies that I used to represent used to assemble hand held and desktop electronic Calculators. Calculators came with multiple features and thus there are number of models to choose from. We found that the entire hand held or pocket calculators were served by the gray market. Our sales were few and those were to a few select institutions that would make a purchase with an official invoice tax paid. We sent the feedback to the company and stopped bringing in those pocket models. However the desktop printer version became our mainstay, though expensive. Computers-PCs- were yet to make an entry and most companies big and small used these printer calculators for their accounting.

My areas of operations were Allahabad in the North to the extreme N.E. region, and down to Vizag in Andhra Pradesh – South. Certain pockets besides Kolkata were reasonably good. The bulk of the business was in Kolkata. The market since then has undergone a sea change. Today many smaller cities and towns in the East are vibrant business centers. Plus a large number of industries have come up in neighboring states with Odisha leading with the second highest FDI investment in the country.

The industrial climate in West Bengal took a nose dive from around 1982. The market refused to grow rather it declined. Bringing in consignments by road was very problematic, harassment at entry point and payment of 'speed money'. Multiple forms needed to be filled and whereas goods would reach Chennai and Delhi in 4 days from Mumbai, here it took 10-15 days. All transporters charged extra, that is over and above the standard transportation rate. They did not do so when transporting to Chennai and Delhi. Cost of landed material became prohibitive. We were forced to bring consignments by air adding to Cost.

I tried to set up a manufacturing unit in Kolkata for a few of the products we were selling in this region. By doing so I could avoid double taxation, freight and the cascade effect of taxes. I was fortunate in having a tie up with some of my principals who were established manufacturers. But the unit I set up here ran into various delays, mainly delays in local government approvals. Some of the objections were laughable. I had asked for permission to manufacture radios. The local SSI department sent the file to the central government for approval. After 9 months I received a letter from the central government that it was within the powers of the local government. What a joke I lost time, market advantage and money. The best part was that the official in charge of the section that dealt with my application could not be taken to task as he was a political functionary.

We are seeing today that mid-sized companies from Europe and the US are setting shop in India and China to leverage manufacturing cost.

Once the West Bengal scenario turned chaotic, companies large and small just left. The joke was, the government said, that these companies are still in Kolkata. The reality was that everyone had moved except the company's name plate. The registered office comprising of one room remained in Kolkata.

The local government having lost in tax revenue started pressurizing small business people. Every month tax inspectors would come not to examine books but asking us to pay advance tax. Advance tax for sales that have not yet taken place. They would average our tax returns for the past two quarters and compute a figure which they would want us to deposit. Noncompliance would mean harassment. It reminded me of the nonsense limericks penned by the noted poet Sukumar Ray[98]. The government needed money to pay salaries.

People in Bengal are culturally inclined. The ambition of an average Bengali is to get a government job, any job, usually clerical – a *babu*. Any other job entails a major evaluation exercise through written and viva. Thus the majority here are 'babus-clerks', whose wish remains till today to travel somewhere with his family during the festival season[99]. Festival bonuses are another big issue. The government too pays a bonus. Why the bonus is paid we who were never in government cannot fathom as employees will never maintain punctuality either in their attendance in the morning or in adhering to closing hours. Bonus issues in non-government sectors led to violence and

[98] Sukumar Ray was the father of the noted film director Satyajit Ray

[99] This is the only state in India where during the Durga Puja holidays all government offices are closed for nearly a week and the Banks for consecutive 3 days.

closures[100]. Carrying on business activities in such a socio-political ecosystem is an art. No amount of management skills taught in B-schools can help.

What can entrepreneurs do in such eventuality? Those who have resources - not only money but good business networks - had already closed shop and moved. Others stayed on as their investments in business, property, the education of their children, their commitment to parents and family elders made such re-location difficult.

In my case, I simply down sized my business and closed shop in various departments with a heavy heart I let go some very good employees. Even now, *I feel the pain of such a parting*. Yet, it took some two years to finally down shutters as government sales tax processes were delayed inordinately; an expense and time which had no financial rewards.

My idea in writing some of these incidents, points at the multi-level planning an entrepreneurial venture need to go into. It is always prudent not to place all the eggs in one basket. When I started out in 1972, I found Kolkata had a vibrant business culture for past 50-60 years. All that changed in the next 12 years or so, who except an astrologer could predict, or may be a far more savvy business man.

---

[100] In addition there are demands for subscriptions from local clubs and political organisations.

Business exodus from a region is akin to deforestations. Once trees are randomly felled, in no time the land turns arid[101]. Reforestation and bringing back fertility is a long tedious and uncertain process. The question, that is foremost in the minds of the people in both such scenarios, what will happen to their livelihood? Probably that's the reason why the locals queue up for a government job 'Aashijai, maine paiye'!![102]

Nobody has an answer. West Bengal not only saw industry disappearing, it continues to witness a steady exodus of the youth in search of better education and jobs in places like Gurgaon, Mumbai, Pune, Bangalore and a few others.

I spent 9 months at Pune University. One can always hear a group chattering away in Bengali, just as one would find in any college in Kolkata. One of the graduates I spoke to has studied in Pune and stayed on alone for the past 8 years. Does she plan to return? No such plans at the moment, though her parents live in Kolkata. There are many like

[101] Without the tree the topsoil which is full of nutrients get depleted. Similarly, without a vibrant economic activity the skilled people migrated in droves. Getting local skilled people in management and technology is proving difficult.

[102] Salary is guaranteed.

her, who comprises the workforce in Pune and other cities across the country.

Coming back to the choice I had in my Business, it took me a year to decide. I carried out a massive reorganization and ventured into health care, an area in which I had no experience what-so-ever I reasoned that the downturn will not adversely affect healthcare business. Not only was it a tough decision, I went through a difficult 2 years during which my business continued to suffer losses.

I could never attain the levels of turnover my earlier business had. When I visit other states and interact with similar healthcare centers that have far fewer facilities and locational advantages than mine, I find their business turnover is way higher. They have far fewer run-ins with the local administration. Yes, I agree that the decision to migrate is a tough personal decision. Many a times this decision is impacted by certain apparently unrelated matters.

Way back in 1974 a company in Kolkata, India started manufacturing voltage stabilizers. A friend of mine was the selling agent for West Bengal. It sounds good, but at that time the product was untested in the market and we were two new entrants in the field of distribution fresh out of college. This was a pretty big organization. My friend and I went to the meeting with their commercial manager who was then in his late 50s. We were both in our early 20s. The very first question was a bouncer for my friend. How is your company constituted? He just froze. Mind you by then he was a graduate in Instrumentation engineering from Jadavpur University.

The first dozen or so units we sold to our friends and acquaintances. They were kind enough to give us very constructive criticism on the product as and when we asked[103]. At times they went overboard with their views. Much later we realized that customers are not techies. They would always ask for facilities that they feel are useful. It is for us to work out a compromise which would benefit the product sales.

Years went by. One day in 1979 we read about a compact player introduced by Sony - Walkman[104]. Sony Walkman was a rage amongst young and old and in later years many other companies came out with their

[103] Two things worried us. One that the unit could just switch off in which case the appliance, usually a refrigerator will stop functioning. Second, if the unit malfunctioned the appliance could get damaged. The second was really worrying.

[104]The prototype was built in 1978 by audio-division engineer Nobutoshi Kihara for Sony co-chairman Akio Morita, who wanted to be able to listen to operas during his frequent trans-Pacific plane trips.[1] The original Walkman was marketed in 1979 as the Walkman in Japan

own versions of Walkman. Subsequently there was the Discman, a compact CD player and today there are various gadgets that store both music and video.

There are a large number of consumer products in the market that were innovated after companies latched on to feedbacks from their customer. Business is market driven

To 'wish' and to 'deliver' are two very different aspects. There have been times that I wished to create a product that I thought my customers demanded. Well in most cases, I was not successful.

By mid 80s 2-in-1, radio and tape recorder combination came into vogue. There was the choice of either buying it from the gray market or buy a poor quality product assembled in India. I tried my best in designing one such that would be comparable to the ones available in the gray market, but failed[105].

For the first two years I was primarily selling entertainment electronics products. After a couple of years I noticed that people were quite harried when it came to servicing these gadgets, or, when they needed some advice on buying additional equipment. A quality home entertainment system is built over time. I was a new entrant with a very modest setup. But I had visited the service centers of

[105] The locally sourced plastic cabinets were of poor quality and obvious poor finish.

some of the better known branded companies in Kolkata. They were appalling. Once I established a reasonably modern service facility, I not only saw an increase of my sales, I earned a fair amount from my service too.

Years after I shut shop, people would come even from other cities and neighboring states looking for service facilities. At times I toyed with the idea of re-starting the service center. But I suppose we all have to move on.

21 SOCIAL ENTREPRENEURSHIP – BUSINESS AND MARKET

- Business is also at the 'Bottom of the Pyramid'
- Build your own personal USP

Some startups in IT that I have come across gravitate towards government business. There are perfectly logical reasons for doing so. First, if one happens to network with a government department, chances are that there is a scope for a reasonable volume of business through a system termed as limited tender. Though at times payments are delayed, but ultimately a payment reaches the company. There is also a chance for a repeat order or an order from another department. Secondly, for newer startups revenue generation is a chicken and egg story. When one approaches a probable customer, invariably he is asked as to who are his clients. This is a very tricky and sometimes embarrassing situation. It immediately places the startup in a defensive wicket. For a startup one customer is a prize.

But for a startup the matter of paramount importance is money. Of course I know a particular case where a state government institution has yet to pay the bill after a year. But usually that's not the case. There are other advantages too[106]. The technical

[106] A major government contract is issued on

specification of a government order does not change in course of the execution of the order. If for some specific reason it is modified, a fresh order with probably new rates are incorporated along with a fresh schedule. That is also an added bonus. In the course of my business I had found that the specifications of such small time contract rarely change over years. Thus if there is a scope for a repeat order, there can be no better business as the next phase probably can be executed with much lesser cost. There is also a possibility of funding from banks on the basis of the order. All in all it is an attractive proposition for a startup.

Is this a 'win – win' situation? I cannot speak for all. In my experience (I was a registered supplier to nearly all major government organizations in the East and some of the corporate houses) I found that once the key person in the office is shunted out, things go crazy. At times I had to spend days trying to figure out who can be approached for a clarification or some support at the client place. It used to be pretty unnerving as my technicians would be idling away and I would be paying for the idling time. There was no way I could bring the matter to a fruitful conclusion unless the officials cooperate. At times I would be so very close to the

the basis of open tender. An open tender is a different ball game altogether. Competing with established players requires much more than cutting edge technology.

deadline, yet my job was far from conclusion. A lot of time needs to be spent in befriending the key person or persons. You must be in a position to get advance information whether the company – translates to the super boss – was in talks with another contractor. If so who? A sort of market intelligence. When my company was small this effort took away a lot of my time.

As I grew I had sales people, not salesmen, given charge of a group of companies each. I had trained them well and I always believed in reporting – one on one and a written report. Every evening I would scrutinize those reports. Every morning there would be a 15 minute briefing.

One of my executives was handling Assam and the NE. We used to get a reasonable level of business from there, but I always thought that we were not up to our potential. I traveled with the guy to Shillong and Guwahati. The flight to Shillong was by a Fokker aircraft which bumped all the way and my executive turned a shade of green. The next was a taxi ride to Guwahati from Shillong. Dusk had already fallen and the driver had imbibed his quota. People in the hills enjoy the tippler. The ride was scary, as the guy drove all through at breakneck speed and my executive kept his eyes closed.

Barring these two glitches we received excellent orders and our clients were extremely happy seeing me around. Even today I cannot forget the hospitality they had extended. I left Guwahati for Kolkata by the evening Indian Airlines flight (those days there were no private airlines). Guwahati airport is quite a distance from downtown and for most parts pretty desolate. The flight was supposed to take off at 5PM. Being the Eastern part of the country, the sunsets early.

Once I reached the airport, I was told that the flight was delayed. Incidentally that was the last flight as in those days Guwahati did not have night landing facilities. I convinced my taxi driver on the promise of additional payment to wait, till I found out whether the flight had actually left Kolkata. Flying time from Kolkata is 55 minutes. Once I received confirmation that it was on the way and expected to land any moment I let the taxi go. I surely was not looking forward to spending the night at the airport. Taxis from the airport to the city were few. Running a business is not easy. It requires a person to be street smart so as to get out of tricky situations. One never knows when such a situation would pop-up.

As I did mention earlier, I had no qualms in supplying to government agencies. However, I never participated in open tenders. Somehow, rightly or wrongly, I never made such large business from single source the mainstay of my business. There was also a matter of funding such large business. I was not a joint stock company. Banks were reluctant to lend large funds. Again one must remember that all the Banks were run by the government. By design my non-government sales were 80%. I was pretty content with what I was doing.

But I did realize that my business volume has reached a plateau. I was looking around for avenues to increase the business. One possibility was to induct partners who would buy equity in my company. But my business associates dissuaded me from doing so, as taking on a person about who little is known in terms of his personal traits and other background leads to untold misery. I have seen that happen. What could be the other alternatives?

One day it suddenly dawned that I could approach my principals with my proposal. There was a hitch. I knew what I wanted. But I had no idea as what would be the business relationship. I took a chance and discussed my idea with one of my principals. He immediately agreed and suggested an acceptable working system. In the next few years I had the opportunity in working closely with some senior leading business people as equals. Of course I always gave them the respect due, as they were my seniors in age and experience.

But all good things come to an end. India's political and economic scenario started deteriorating from 1988 and by 1991 the government of India was hocking India's gold reserves to avoid sovereign default. Soon thereafter the dam burst and the government announced opening up to overseas companies. We had 2 Prime Ministers in a period of 2 years. Opening up or liberalization is a welcome policy. But the local industry had no time to strategies for the onward march of global giants. Indian companies of all shades fell like nine pins. The same fate befell my principals and obviously it affected me badly.

The critical difference between an entrepreneur and a job seeker is that a chap out of job hunts for one and has the choice of accepting one even though the salary may not be as per expectation. For the entrepreneur, the loss of business also translates to loss of money. Hunting for fresh capital is a tough ask. If the guy has a god-father he could sail through.

Fortunately, I had a bit of kitty, not much. I shifted through various ideas and settled on expanding my health care business. My experience in health care helped me to take into account the fact that positive revenue generation needs at least two to two and half years. Well I took the plunge and it has worked. I did not approach financial institutions for funds. My companies though small have no creditors.

A startup in the knowledge domain has the ability in providing quite a few products and services that have varied utility. But as we all know it is not possible to develop all these together. The choice of product or service needs to be narrowed down to the level of possibility of execution by the startup team.

The market out there is massive. Actually the market is a grand feast. As in any grand feast we tend to gravitate towards those items that we prefer and ignore the rest. Big names McDonalds', Subway, Nokia, Blackberry, Nike, GE and a host of others have made their presence felt in the past couple of decades in the Indian market. These companies have spent considerable time in testing the market. In a particular case I was told that the guys came in five years prior to the date they actually opened for business.

There can be no comparison as far as resources as men, material and money is concerned. During the same period that these giants set up shop, quite a few big brands did exit the Indian market. Generally the companies that did exit happened to leave in the first 10 years of the new policy of 1991. I had not followed up on those exiting, and cannot elucidate. Even in the last ten years global companies have wound up. Daewoo the manufacturer of the Matiz car in India went bankrupt and the owners of those vehicles find it extremely difficult to get spares. Mortality is part of the scene. One has to be prepared for such eventuality in business. With some preparation the shock is bearable. Thus after a hiatus, it is very much possible to spring back. Let us all understand that the experience, any experience in business is worth its weight in gold.

An off shoot of the global brands' entry has been their skill in reaching the markets of Tier II cities. Arguably, this has brought a certain sense of inclusiveness. Who would have thought of air-conditioned shopping malls in smaller cities? Who would have thought of such shopping malls sporting grand food courts? Without doubt it brings in a sense of cheer in the people. I would always vote for a system whereby people living away from major cities feel that they too have recourse to things that a city dweller has.

One thing comes out loud and clear. The opportunity in the Indian market place is in 'inclusion'. I will urge startups to take a close look at this issue. I have mentioned earlier that the bulk of startups are in IT services. IT services generally are business that is dependent on overseas clients. Even after years in business any economic downturn in the country of the client, sends shockwaves in Indian companies. We must find ways and means within the country to ride such shocks. My logic is if companies have gone ahead and setup extensive infrastructure for their business here in India, it is obvious that they have identified their market. I would urge Indian startups to do the same. Being Indians we are better placed to understand local needs. Let us seriously make an effort to explore these right at home.

There is no cause to lose heart if there happens to be a downturn. It is like a modern aircraft with the latest in avionics. In spite of that the aircraft does develop snags. It is up to the two pilots up there to take the controls and safely land the aircraft. And in most cases they are successful. In business the team is in control, through systems in place. If there is a problem you take the decision to take charge at the most appropriate time. And I am sure it will help your business to ride out the storm.

This business flip flop also brings with it a lot of data. It is important to keep a record of what one learns in the process. Some if not all the data will help you to further strengthen your business plan. The business plan is not a static document. And please see to it that the plan does not stagnate.

In the Indian context business is regularly battered by changing government regulations generally arising out of some concurrent political issues. We have seen it happening in Kolkata when AMRI a 1000 bed hospital caught fire (in 2011, leading to some 80 people perishing in the fire). Immediately the government clamped down on all nursing homes. I am all for strict rules especially for health care. The fact is the rules are there but its adherence has been a problem. The question is why. It is for the administration to put a system in place which is uniformly applied to all. Any laxity in administration leads to complications, which in turn leads to loss in the economy. Yes, as in all spheres of activity there are people who break the law. But it would not stand to reason that everybody breaks the law. It is not only a loss for the business also for citizens who need the services.

I interact with a fairly good numbers of

techies who have graduated from some of the leading academic institutions of the country. Many of their ideas have developed from the academic programs they had attended. In quite a few cases they have also developed miniature models that were displayed at their science fairs. But scale models and business or two separate ends of a long pole. As far as their product goes, in most cases I have found those to be promising. But one cannot just hope to become a contractor to the Indian Space Research Organization the leading agency that places satellites in orbit.

But what is the probability factor?

Let the startup act local to begin with. Acting local does not preclude the startup from looking at the global scenario. It does not stop them in strategizing for the global market. The act 'local' helps bring revenue quicker. It will also help the company in gaining 'experience' in the market place. Like a child the business must in stages gear up. It cannot become a long distance runner on the very first day or the very first year.

22 THE CUSTOMER

- *"A customer is the most important visitor on our premises. He is not dependent on us. We are dependent on him. He is not an interruption of our work. He is the purpose of it. He is not an outsider of our business. He is part of it. We are not doing him a favor by serving him. He is doing us a favor by giving us the opportunity to do so."* – M. K. Gandhi, 1890 in South Africa
- Educate your intended customer on your product and services
- Go the Extra Mile
- Why the government of India could not run one single business profitably in a monopoly market from 1947-1992?

For any entrepreneur the customer is the king! At least they should be the king. It is often said that if you make your customer feel like a king he will end up spending like a king. But to treat a customer as a king need not mean that you just massage his ego. Of course you will try to make him feel comfortable about the product or service you are offering. But beyond that what a customer often expects from you is proper guidance and some integrity. They see you as the expert and seek your help to make an informed choice. An entrepreneur must always remember that at the end of the day, no matter how innovative his product, the customer needs to be convinced to pay for it. In this chapter we look at some of the key things to remember when dealing with your customers.

Inform and Educate Your Customer

The buyer is a person who has his own preferences, which depends on various factors – need, budget, may be a specific occasion, social occasions as in weddings, etc. Add to this the overall situation in the neighborhood, the sudden emergencies that the family may be facing like health issues and/or immediate expenses towards children's education.

Business and its success depend on perception. Would you try a packet of biscuits which has a name printed that you have never heard of? People want our services only when they have a perception that this venture has been around for some time. A sort of guarantee of quality. In India, we are extremely wary of 'fly by night' operators[107].

Once I paid Rs.500/- by mail order for a list of vendors' name. After a month (by then I had lost hope of receiving any such list) I received a CD which had a list of vendors with incomplete names in some cases, and with incomplete address in others.

While planning marketing strategy, it is very important that our intended customer can access the company profile and take a look at the people who run the show. I see a number of websites, quite well presented, offering various services. When I try to find out as to who the people are offering such services, I hit a brick wall. Why hide? If business has to succeed, one must come out on the street and be visible – learn from the street vendors. I really want to know why the websites do what they do.

We hear of ideas and innovations that cater to 'niche' market. To my mind there is nothing 'niche' about market. In Kolkata, one of the scions of a business house opened a high class boutique. Every day when I used to pass by I would wonder, what probably could be their USP. After a few years the person closed shop. Frankly, I do not know why the owners opened it in the first place and why did it close down. One thing I do recollect is that no one in my network ever mentioned the shop in any of our discussions. Of course in India, many such

---

[107]Except in Ponzi schemes. I am really amazed how the same people who are so conscious about product and quality succumb to 'greed'.

businesses are established to get a tax break. I believe a sensible business should rather increase their profits, pay taxes and create wealth. The company Steve Jobs founded had a cash reserve of $75b in 2011. Apple did not reach such height through tax breaks. Why can we not aim for something similar?

The other related issue I have seen is the propensity of the entrepreneur in forcing a point of view on to the customer. Generally, it is about his innovation. This is an absolute no, no. Just an example will suffice. Frequent air travelers have a distinct inclination towards a certain carrier. Some would prefer Continental, others Lufthansa. Both these companies are pretty efficient and are established brands. But the market has its own thoughts on these.

While in the music system business, I had many such experiences. Before discrete stereo systems hit the market, radiogram was in vogue. Usually these were ornate wooden cabinets (sometimes very garish) fitted with a radio, record player and loud speakers. Actually, at medium to high volume the entire cabinet used to vibrate.

Many of our customers were disappointed when they saw our discrete system of record players, amplifiers and loudspeakers. Some remarked that these would make their home take a marriage hall ambience.

We had to come out with a combo – a record

player and amplifier combined. The speakers were separately attached that did help to some extent.

The other issue was the matter of the hi-fidelity. Gramophone and radiograms have limited audio frequency ranges – lo-fidelity. Thus, the bass would be very prominent. Our customers were used to listening to the limited audio range and attuned to the 'boomy' bass. When they heard true hi-fidelity some did not like the higher range response, they called it 'teeny' sound and some thought that the audio response was not balanced. By that they really meant that it did not sound true. We had a trying few years in teaching our customers the use of tone controls (graphic equalizers, as it is called now). Looking back, I think it was fun.

Our amplifiers were rated at 100 watts, 200 watts, etc. These were the output power of the main amplifier. Customers would come with a 100 w electric bulb and ask us to show them that the amplifier was really a 100 w one, by lighting their electric bulb.

At no point can the entrepreneur reject the opinion of the customer. Dealing with varied feedback from the market allows us to hone our skills that normally we do not acquire in our colleges. We probably do not remember our own off-the-cuff remarks of a dish served at home, that for some reason we did not like. Did we ever think of the hurt it caused to the lady of the house? Well, the market place comprises people whom we have never met, and probably comes from a background quite at variance with ours. Their remarks can be far more acidic.

Going the Extra Mile

Whatever may be the type of business one may be in, there must be something extra that the business must provide to its customers. Some companies do provide the add-ons. But in reality, I found that most of these facilities have a hidden cost built-in. It has been my experience that such means create a negative impact.

Some companies are of the opinion that as a business house they cannot provide charity. True. But the company will in the medium term gain substantially by increase of sales through the level of trust and bonding it builds with its customers. It is a proven fact that no amount of overt publicity can achieve what the word of mouth can.

In return, as a consumer, I feel a certain level of gratitude for having being directed in the right or possibly the best solutions for my need.

Consumers in urban areas are aware of their rights. What is most appalling is that more and more financial institutions – banks, insurance companies – are locked in disputes in consumer courts. I was quite surprised when an FM channel started announcing a court order awarded in favor of the consumer against a bank that had refused to pay interest on a sum of money citing some rules[108]. Corporate social responsibility is a joke. The top notch honchos of corporates love to wax and wane on the CSR at various forums. But they never fault their own companies in service deficiencies[109].

I would like to emphasize this issue. A large number of startups are in 'services'; this is an area that brings in returns faster than say manufacturing, training, cultivation (as in agriculture). Customers are looking for 'dependable' service providers. We all are aware that known brands are not necessarily dependable. As I have mentioned earlier in my book, a brands brings in a sense of security for the customer. Unfortunately, as far as service goes, a brand is not a guarantee. Many of us have found that out much to our distress. Yes, we could approach the courts. But we all have a certain level of

[108] Just a couple of years ago if a customer forgot to renew his FD, the bank would refuse to pay any interest from the period on which the FD ought to have been renewed till the date of actual renewal. No one looked into the fact that the all the time the money was lying in the bank, till an aggrieved customer took the matter to court.

[109] On the social network site, FB, I followed the experience of a consumer who had bought a refrigerator for nearly INR 60,000/- After the product was delivered he found that it was defective. It took him one month to get a replacement. That's the CSR on the ground.

commitment as a wage earner. To add to our daily stress is not a very attractive proposal. I think companies are aware of the hurdles that their distressed customers face in taking recourse to courts. They are also aware few will ever take recourse to the legal process.

Many of us, therefore, utilize the services of small-time service provider. I have been using one such for all my computer-related issues right from 1998. I am savvy about computers. But I find it difficult to spare the time and shop for what I need, may be toners, a cable, or an additional peripheral. And I am quite happy with his services.

A customer is primarily looking for a need to be served. Next in line is his comfort zone. For example, how many would buy a TV set without a remote. Some years back there used to be a price difference of about R 1500 between the two. Today, all manufacturers have incorporated the remote control, as the consumer preference has changed. Times have changed – from formals to T-shirts and jeans, from a packed lunch to pasta or pizza lunch. Yes, someone has really read the change.

Number of startups are in the knowledge domain. And they are technology driven enterprises. It is decidedly true that technology drives the business model better and *at times faster*. I want to add a caution that too much credence on the ability of technology can actually drive the business off its rails.

Let us recollect that the Bullet train with the latest technology – a wonder when it was introduced – still needs someone to be up there to keep a watch on the systems. I used to wonder why the train could not be run by remote as they do in city metros. It is too much of a risk. Even with such advanced technologies there are imponderables.

How important is the human touch? In December 2011, Best Buy USA started refusing delivery of merchandise to its customers who had already bought the product online. Don't ask me how could they do so? Soon the management realized the blunder and scrambled to rectify the same, by reaching out to every one of its customers. What a goof up? It seems the supply chain went haywire. Mind you, outlets like Best Buy, Macys and others run the entire business on a 'sound' supply chain management system. But technology does fail. It is the human touch that comes forth to retrieve the situation.

It is my belief that stabilizing the business activities of a startup once it has started generating revenue is far more difficult than actually starting off. It reminds me of the experiment in physics where on stretching a wire it ultimately reaches its point of elasticity. Business operations at times get stretched. It takes a lot of skill not to cross the point of elasticity. For startups with little experience they fail to identify the point and thus reach a point of no return. That I would say is where a mentor steps in and does a hand holding[110].

Managing an enterprise is the key. This statement is also a cliché. But is it management and nothing else? I am of the view that the owners develop a misplaced pride when their business starts flourishing – generating revenue. This misplaced pride makes them pompous[111]. Startups, as I said earlier, must shun their egos. The feet need to be firmly placed on the *terra firma*. One slip and one falls on the face. Your attitude in an enterprise is replicated all the way down. The same attitude one sees in government bureaucrats and their minions in India. Ask your selves what sort of respect do you have for these officials? At the same time I fail to understand why the officials behave the way they do as most come from social backgrounds of the Indian middle class. And by and large the middle class bring to the civil society its human touch.

Am I being a moralistic preacher? Till a time I was only an entrepreneur I accepted the attitude of the officials. Pre-liberalization my seniors in business always advised me not to

[110] See the role of the Mentor

[111] It is a common belief in India that a running business would head for collapse once the controls pass from the founders to their children. And there are countless such examples.

get too close to them, neither should I ever create issues with them, whatever may be the rules that the bureaucrat may be violating. The reasoning was that the time spent in such wrangling could be better spent in one's own business. Probably it's true. But it is also true that this has given rise to a high level of dishonesty in public life.

For nearly 14 years I took on assignment in academic and research institutions (most of them government run institutions). At that point I was sitting on the other side of the table. For the first time I used to feel uncomfortable. Later, I worked out a system whereby I tried to make my visitor comfortable. However, once you hold such a position a number of people come to meet you. Most did not know that I am actually an entrepreneur. They would act in the same way as one did when visiting senior government officials. There were many invites. Let me not describe them. But instead of getting angry I used to be amused. Later, they shared with me experiences with other officials of the institute. What made me sad that some senior officials, definitely not all, put their reputation on the line. After all they were members of the respected teaching community, a community that we look up to.

What a shame!

A concern for your customers can create magic for your sales. I cannot detail the approach one needs to take. But essentially there needs to be a genuine concern. Probably one approach could be to put yourself in your customers'[112] shoes.

My health care facility is a small establishment though located very centrally in Kolkata. We have people visiting us from all parts of Kolkata and sometimes from other cities too. The clinic remains closed from 1PM-4PM (The timings have since changed). However I have instructed my security to let people in if they arrive before 4PM. Waiting on the curb side in summer is extremely unpleasant especially when they have children with them. Plus someone in that group is obviously sick. That is the very purpose of their visit. I think this is the least we can do – provide a comfortable waiting space and the use of rest rooms.

To check whether my staffs do open the gate on time, or whether they have allowed the patient inside before 4PM, I make surprise

[112] I had a trying time to get a refund from an Insurance company. After I had filed a complaint with IRDA a lady from the company called me. Till such time nobody bothered to check with me or reply to my emails. I told the lady without raising my voice that did she realise what can happen to her once she left the company for some better opportunity elsewhere. Would she want to be treated the way I am? She immediately became very apologetic. I think all that is needed is a bit of 'concern'. One never knows when the shoe is on the other foot.

visits to my clinic. It is not enough to give instructions. One must make certain that instructions are being followed. Large companies at times with all fancy systems in place miss out the fact that there are people at every critical junction who need to be supervised.

For the past few years we keep hearing of various disturbances at various health centers in the city and the state. Fortunately in the past 25 years we did not have to face such a situation. This is not to say that it cannot happen in future. But we do make an effort to provide minimum basic facilities for our visitors. Normally, the waiting time is not more than half an hour. May be the visitors too try to keep their cool. The eco-system is such that a small incident can create a chaos as poor health care facility in the state has made people edgy.

23 THE TARGET GROUPS

Kolkata has had the famous eatery Nizam's. We used to flock to Nizam's when in college for their famous *kati rolls*. I have used the past tense not because the eatery does not exist today, but it has re-invented itself after a hiatus of nearly two decades. Today, their Rolls are nowhere near what it used to be earlier. I am told the cooks of yester years have all left.

What is a 'kati roll'? It is a paratha[113] with a filling of one's choice – chicken, fish, paneer, kebabs or simply boiled potatoes with egg and garnished with sliced onion, green chilies, a few drops of lemon juice and a special seasoning, rolled up. We all felt that the paratha was so unique and the kebabs were to die for. I remember one guy would just fry the paratha and leave it for another chap to complete the process of the wrap.

[113] Fried Indian Roti like Bread.

Years later after the joint had closed down (communist militant labor agitation) a few of their workers started a small eatery just on the pavement outside the place. I was thrilled to see the assistant of the erstwhile paratha cook preparing the paratha and as per convention he left it for another chap to complete the formalities. And I believe that paratha was out of the world.

There are a number of anecdotes on this kati roll. One that appealed to me goes as follows.

The Kolkata Mounted Police headquarters are located very close to this eatery. During the British rule the Sergeant – a white man – leading the early morning recce would drop in for his morning grub of Paratha and kebabs. One morning the Sergeant was in a hurry. He hollered at the owner – *Jaaldi Koro*[114]. He wanted the food to be served while on horseback. The poor guy quickly found a solution. He unloaded the kebabs on the Paratha with the usual salad of sliced onion and green chillies, rolled it up in a jiffy and scrambled to the Sergeant. The Sergeant was mighty pleased with the new dish and subsequently, every day he would ask for the 'kati roll'. 'Kati' in Hindi denotes the wooden skewers that were used to grill the meat. Multiple versions of this Roll are today sold across the country. But none to beat the one of the yester-years' Nizam's.

---

[114] Hurry up!!

I could not think of any other innovation in modern times that has not undergone any further modification in the past 80 years[115]. The roll is a snack that pleases the Indian palate, unlike a burger. It is eater friendly and can be had –sitting, standing and walking. Since the fillings are dry there is no mess – no sauces that tend to drip or smear the face. The only thing that needs discarding is the small piece of paper that is used to pack the roll.

Is it just one of those things that do happen? Things that we cannot explain? Or just like Steve Jobs and his iPhone, was this a touch of genius by the cook-cum-owner of Nizam's? I would cast my vote for sheer mastery of the owner in dishing out an extremely innovative food item in its new avatar in a jiffy. Unfortunately he had never heard of patent laws. By now he could have become a millionaire many times over.

What I have been writing about in the last few pages has been about the need for startups in connecting with target groups. It

[115] Having said that, the cane juice cart we see in every city is another innovative product that has caught the imagination of the people of the country. It is a very popular drink, in spite of all the dust and pollutants the juice ingest while on the road. Unfortunately, I could not find any reference to by whom or where this contraption was innovated.

is not technology alone that can carry the enterprise through. You will realize that parathas and kebabs are a very common item in many Indian household. It is available in the smallest of *dhabas* and roadside eateries in India. Sure, Nizam's is reputed for its food. What the eatery could do was raise the bar by its sheer competence in delivery. Without this 'kati-roll', this eatery would have been like any other.

Ask any old timer visiting Kolkata during the 50s, 60s and the early part of 70s a visit to Nizam's was a must on their itinerary. Kolkata port was abuzz with ships lined up on the Ganges awaiting berth at the Kidderpur docks. Nizam's was a favourite with the sailors. It reminded me of a pilgrimage. How did all the folks on the ships, of various nationalities ever hear of a small eatery in Kolkata? Yet, the fact that they did visit it by droves proves that the eatery went global without a single ad in any newspaper, magazine or even a write up in the New York Times.

Business is about people. Any startup must have realized it by now. We love to talk global. If we intend interacting with people of other countries, it is very important that our cultures have a meeting point. Small innocuous personal traits matter a lot. I am of the view that if we could rectify or at least be conscious of our personal habits that are a strict no no, 70% of the battle is won. And let me clarify, I am not talking of European countries or the USA. The business culture is fairly standard and practiced in all South East

Asian countries, Africa and the Middle East.

During one of my visits to the USA as a part of the Indian delegation, we were invited to the residence of our host for an evening. Wine and beer along with various tit-bits were served. It was a wonderful evening with an opportunity of networking with delegates from other countries. The house became a bit too crowded, but again no jostling. A few from our team did not partake in the wine. That is quite acceptable.

However, one of our team members thought it was a tourist destination and he ought to carry out a recce. Somehow he overlooked the fact that the house was a home of our host and we ought to be maintaining a certain decorum which I am sure ought not to be part of a briefing. To cut the long story short, I requested his colleague to immediately get him back to where we all stood. What was interesting was his utter lack of any guilt. In India we call this '*Jai Ho*'! Looking back I laugh at it for the hush hush manner we went about getting the guy back. It reminds of a probable scene from a cheap Bollywood flick.

I am sure if you reflect on your own experiences some nuggets would emerge. I only hope that when we speak of India as the global destination (which I presume includes Chinese enterprises too), we are not looking forward to business people changing their attire to dhoti and kurta along with a chappal and a tin of *pan masala* in their hand. Lord forbid! At the same time let the serious folks go all out in making India the favored destination.

24 BUSINESS IS ABOUT PEOPLE

Economists are the modern day 'gurus'. Every day the media would have some one or the other quoting some economists on the state of the global economy. For the past decade India and China have received high accolades. Unfortunately, in the past four years rating agencies have kept downgrading the sovereign rating of India till in 2012 it has given the country a negative outlook. We do have some people who are experts in bluster. Are they paid for being what they are? I wonder. So the blustering people came forth with their view that S&P's rating does not bother us. If so then why talk about it. Why call the print media and issue a correction? Amazing things keep happening.

I was a keen follower of Alan Greenspan, the former chairman of the US Federal Reserves. I am given to understand that Mr. Greenspan has been the only official who has been felicitated by both the US house of lawmakers. I had finished three fourth of his book[116] when the news of the collapse of Lehman Brothers hit the ceiling. The world stank.

I stopped reading the book. How could a man with the most intimate knowledge of the US economy not know that one year down the line the economy of the country will tank? It reminds me of Nero! I think the greatest tragedy was that of the US lawmakers getting carried away by a well-practiced script[117] which was more like a lullaby. What a tragedy!

Immediately, people in the US and elsewhere including our own started finding faults with the US system. They coined words like greed, criminal intent, and others. Those in other countries acted 'holier than thou'. In a short span every country was reeling under the effects of this meltdown.

The US had gone through quite a few roller coasters and the great depression of the '30s is still fresh in memory. But as a country it

[116] The Age of Turbulence

[117] How could people in the US, the regulators not know of subprime scams? A year before the bubble burst, BBC carried a TV show that depicted as humor as to what was happening in the mortgage market.

has the resilience in riding the worst scenario. I believe, even after the meltdown, it remains the strongest economy in the world.

It is the people of the country who have made what the US is today. The settlers were there much before Adam Smith. They made the country a global power. It is a country where the settlers have arrived and many are still endeavoring to go to, from every corner of the globe. I believe these immigrants have it in them to make it big.

In my writings I keep harping on people. Well, startups too are people. The knowledge startups have brought forth an Innovative way to become an entrepreneur – the mind – or what we now term as intellectual property.

I am not saying that in the earlier days entrepreneurs were people who did not apply their minds. That's not true. However, in earlier days business generally evolved around a product – a machine, land building, eatery, road transport, air transport. It still does. Those are some of the major investment areas in most countries.

However, today an entrepreneur needs only a table, chair, a computer with internet connectivity to start off. That is a far cry from an earlier business structure. The nearest one can compare with would have been an insurance agent. But I don't think any insurance agent has ever made it as big as Bill Gates or Steve Jobs. That makes all the difference. Plus the new-age startup is absolutely mobile. Today, a lot of business takes place on the coffee shop table, with some notes scribbled on paper napkins. And these deals are at times in millions of dollars. A conference today is carried out anywhere - car, airport, roadside you name it. A repeated phrase one hears – let me patch the guy in. That is one of the caller's calls up someone else and connects him to the conference. Connectivity – both voice and data – is seamless.

Yet we do need people to network, whether by conference calls, emails or video chat. All the latest gizmos cannot replace the person. Yes, business is about people.

I was recently watching a television show in which the presenter was depicting the Grand Bazar of Istanbul. The Bazar has 3600 shops under one roof. A shopkeeper made a telling point on business being done with love and feeling. We must love what we are doing. As I have mentioned earlier, the business cannot be only about 'money making'. The business must take cognizance of the probable customer and such love and feeling will translate to a sale as the customer too would be a partner in the process. Try it and you will get results.

One must have feeling for the wares on sale. The product on sale must take on the care that we the makers have bestowed on it. At the same time we must see to it that the customer's[118] need is fulfilled. At times the product on sale is of top most quality, but it is not what the customer needs. If we want 'satisfied' customers, this part of the business is of paramount 'interest'.

[118] Joshua Bell the virtuoso violinist played six Bach pieces using a $ 3.5m violin on the NY subway. A minute later, the violinist received his first dollar tip: a woman threw the money in the till and without stopping continued to walk.

A few minutes later, someone leaned against the wall to listen to him, but the man looked at his watch and started to walk again. Clearly he was late for work.

The one who paid the most attention was a three-year old boy. His mother tagged him along, hurried but the kid stopped to look at the violinist. Finally, the mother pushed hard and the child continued to walk turning his head all the time. This action was repeated by several other children. All the parents, without exception, forced them to move on.

In the 45 minutes the musician played, only six people stopped and stayed for a while. About 20 gave him money but continued to walk their normal pace. He collected $32. When he finished playing and silence took over, no one noticed it. No one applauded, nor was there any recognition.

Obviously, if Bell was looking at enlightened listeners, the subway was not the place or was it?

Today, mail order is big business. Companies such as Amazon, I understand, lead globally. A decade or so back we were wary of ordering anything by mail order. Twice having ordered, I found the product to be not of the quality I had hoped for. The companies never responded to a complaint. Neither did they ask for customer feedback. But that has not been the case when I ordered in the past two years through the same mail order system online. There is also the facility for returning the goods. Today's customer is savvier and companies understand the markets better. As the Turkish shopkeeper mentioned, every customer of his comes back with two other customers. His shop is now being run by the third generation. He claimed that he never worries about money. Can business be carried out in any other way?

One day a few minutes after we opened for business, an officer of the Indian Air Force walked in. He had carried with him a stereo amplifier for repairs. As usual, our service department made the necessary entry. However, the gentleman wanted the set to be set right that very day. The problem was that we had a system of FIFO[119] and already the other customers have been intimated of their delivery dates.

My service department guy came over to

---

[119] First In First Out

discuss the issue with me. I realized that this must be some special case. I went out to meet the person. He told me that he was from the Indian Air Force Base at Jorhat, Assam. I told him about our problem. He just told me that at the Air Base Officers Club the music system was the only entertainment the officer look forward to in the evenings. He has arrived that morning in a fighter aircraft. The aircraft was on standby at the airbase to fly him back. He further told me this was also a request from the CO.

I could say nothing further. I requested him to be seated and offered him some refreshment. We could repair the set by 2 PM. In the intervening period not once did he bother us. Our worry was that at times the equipment fails during the final 'load' test. In such an eventuality we will not be in a position to deliver it the same day. All our staff felt a sense of satisfaction once we could complete the job.

Some 10 days later we received a letter from the CO[120] expressing his thanks and those of his fellow officers. For a pretty long time I had displayed the letter on our notice board. That is what brings in a sense of satisfaction in business. I wish I had preserved the communication and would have been in a position to share it with my readers. At that time we felt a quiet satisfaction for having done a small bit for our brave army men manning the inhospitable forward bases. These men help us to sleep peacefully at

[120] Commanding Officer

night.

I am sure many of the entrepreneurs have such unique experiences. It must have given them a similar sense of satisfaction. I feel such incidents help the entrepreneurs overcome challenges that they face in course of running their enterprises. Many of us want to contribute to the betterment of the civil society through our enterprises. Each of us tries to achieve goals that are unique. I can give many examples of people trying to do so. But it does not always translate to something meaningful. But the energy and efforts in achieving such goals are laudable. Sure acknowledgement makes one feel good. But the goal is not about receiving the accolades. That needs to be clear. It is about building an institution that has the hallmark of the builder.

25 BUSINESS AND ETHICS

- A business that has mopped up a large amount of money from the people by false promise. – Chit Funds.
- In spite of various scams that regularly appear in the media there are large numbers who are gullible and invest their hard earned wealth
- Is this the Knowledge Enterprise of the 21st century?

An enterprise in the knowledge domain is essentially an initiative in providing the civil society a service/product with a cutting edge technology. Unless people feel a need, there can be no market. New product or service (apps is the modern jargon) can be beneficial to people. But not necessarily so. Companies have been known to promote various games which the children and even adults find very addictive. The business of finding newer games to be marketed is a big business today. There are multiple social tensions that rise from such products.

At the same time tablets are reckoned to be useful products, which have games as applications. For that matter, any ordinary mobile application has a few games stored in it. It is difficult to answer a question whether such apps are useful to the society. I frankly don't know. Probably one way of looking at it could be that it keeps the individual busy at a time when the person has time to kill.

Having said this, there are umpteen products today in the market that surely brings a degree of relief in the routine drudgery. These include

- Microwave ovens
- Induction hotplates
- Timers
- Alarms
- Programmable devices for carrying out a host of routine functions.
- Anti-collision devices for vehicles
- GPS
- And many more

I do not think the inventor of the mobile phone ever realized that his first product in 1973 after four iterations by Motorola would one day change the way the people of the world communicate. Number of mobile phones in use in India is 886 million[121]. Indeed a staggering figure in a nation with a population of 1.2billion.

---

[121] Wikipedia June, 2011 fig.

Mobile phones became popular after the price of the instrument dropped post 2000 and subsequently the service providers dropped their call charges substantially.

Before 2000 Indians had to go through a grueling time in getting a landline connection from the government monopoly telephone company. Further, the service provided was extremely poor. The process was riddled with high-handedness and corruption[122].

Outside metro cities, getting access to a working telephone was a matter of luck. It was also a matter of concern when people travelled to such places for business or pleasure. Today all this has changed. We are update on absolute real time basis as to where a person is, whether boarding an aircraft or on a train or bus. In our social system, the mobile phone is the only savior.

Would the world be a better place without the mobile communication? I do not think so. But the same cannot be said of all the other gadgets/bonds[123] that have now flooded the market. The signals for businesses are confusing to say the least. We were confronted with the meltdown in the biggest financial market in 2008. A respected

[122] The TV channel has a satire named 'Ulta Pulta'. There were quite a few episodes on the working of the telephone department.

[123] The subprime scam in the US is a case in point. So are the various 'Chit Funds' in India that operate under very lax controls.

bank, Lehman Brothers, closed shop. The global economy went in a tailspin. We saw fraudster like Madoff being sentenced to 150 years in prison. In India, a cabinet minister has been in prison on charges of fraud[124] that is claimed to be the biggest in Indian history.

A question that immediately comes to mind is what actually happened? Did a meteor hit our global economy? Yes, there has been some analysis. Junk bonds were promoted and sold to investors. I can only share the pain of the thousands of ordinary folks holding on to worthless paper in which they have invested their life savings.

In India, which had a predominately government monopoly in the financial sector[125], Unit Scheme 1964 would have been revealed to be a scam sometime in end 2001, but for the intervention of the Government of India[126]. People did lose a lot of money. At that point, I remember, pensioners who had most of the saving in Units were devastated. And I don't think anybody was prosecuted.

---

[124] It is a rarity in India. Fraud cases drag on for years. And people forget.

[125] Till the 90s.

[126] Unit Scheme-1964: betraying public trust- Source: Mutualfundsindia.com Research Team. The scheme has since been revamped and now works under stringent controls.

Now, once again, the mutual fund is being aggressively promoted. Do we, the common people, have any clue on the working of these mutual funds? They use a sophisticated instrument, modern technology and pretty impressive jargons and legalese to promote themselves. We have business papers where apparently experts wax and wane on the economy. Yet, when markets drop all of a sudden, as it happened in September, 2011[127], the same experts run for cover.

One must always take the views of such analysts with a large pinch of salt. People have a penchant for quick and easy money. While "sweepstakes" and "betting's" are under strict government controls, I find that mutual fund and the stock markets are still evolving. Even with apparently the finest fiscal regulations, the recent sentencing of Rajaratnam, the owner of Galleon in the USA, Rajat Gupta one time director at Goldman Sachs, show the sort of manipulation that exists even in the most developed nations of the world.

The Indian financial system, to my mind, is still in its formative stages. The downgrading of State Bank of India[128] is a matter of great

---

[127] As this book is going through a final review in Aug 13, the Indian economy has tanked. Nobody in the Federal government is ready to come forth with a credible solution.

[128]On October 4, Moody's — one of the big three rating agencies, Standard & Poor's and Fitch Ratings being the other rating agencies —

concern. Days after it was downgraded, the bank requested the government for infusion of funds. Our fiscal system needs transparency. Financial instruments are complicated, and for the common man opaque. The smart selling techniques and highlighting the growth of selected scrips brings in a sense of *déjà vu.*

Under the present dispensation, public companies present their balance sheets once a year. An abstract unaudited account is presented every quarter. How many investors know how to read a balance sheet? The Satyam scandal also shows that leading auditors are in cahoots with crooked dealings of firms. The regulatory body of the chartered accountants needs to be spruced up. It is also to be remembered that this fraud was never detected by any regulatory agencies and there are multiple in play – the CBDT, RBI, CLB, ED, Foreign Exchange Regulator and a few move.

This is worrying. Yes, greed is a termite that could destroy the economic and moral fiber of any nation. We must have a thought process in place to counter **greed**.

The success of a business is the trust that it

reduced its rating on SBI's financial strength (basically credit worthiness) from C minus to D plus amidst concerns over deteriorating asset quality and adequacy of capital. – The Hindu Oct 16, 2011 holds in the market. We have discussed the *essentiality of need, the scourge of greed* and now the crucial element to help build *a good business is need.* As I have mentioned throughout, we need to constantly focus on the broad picture. Since we deal with people, the society, the eco-system is quite blurred. Our building blocks, the foundation thereof, must be rock solid. This stable structure can only be created through a long-term goal of earning the trust of our customers.

ABOUT THE AUTHOR

Arindam Dutta's activities are varied. A first generation entrepreneur he started his entrepreneurial initiatives end 1972 while studying for his master's program at BHU, India. During this journey there were times when he thought that the business would fold up. Yet he believed in his dream - Never say, Die!!

From 1998, he had been an Advisor and Board member at Science Parks and Incubators located in leading Indian academic Institutions– IIT Kharagpur, Bref Biotech, Kharagpur, CMERI (R&D ,CSIR), Durgapore, Innovation Park, MMRDA, Mumbai and others.

His greatest compliments have been from his startups, some have graduated from the institutes where he was involved. They keep in touch.

He is a frequent speaker at leading academic institutions and forums in the world including India. He was invited as a Judge for the Intel Berkeley Technology Entrepreneurship Challenge at UC B, California in 2007. Seven top level VC fund managers were the other members of the panel. Spending a day with people who have funded some of the most successful ventures in the world has been a lifetime experience. For the past three years I am also on the Mentors' panel for 'Power of Ideas' a Business Plan competition conducted by the Economic Times group of Newspapers. He has conducted workshops on Innovation & Entrepreneurship at Universities in Oman in 2012 and 2013. The Times of Oman covered the program in their news.

He continues doing what he knows best – his entrepreneurial activities. His interest areas are alive through the mentoring initiatives as a consultant. In 201I one of my team won the EMTEC TR-35 social entrepreneur of the year challenge and the other won the Texas A&M-Lockheed Martin Challenge. For more on my activities please visit www.startupfacilitator.com.

Annex 52

LETTER OF GRATITUDE

To
The Program Coordinator
Entrepreneurship Development Program
St. Xavier's College,
Kolkata.

Dear Sir,

This is to bring into your kind notice, that we had the most wonderful privilege of undergoing an eight week training program at the **Biochemistry Department** of **Ballygunge Science College**. To begin with, we would term this training as a big success. Thereby we would extend our heartiest gratitude to our honorable Dr. Santasree Mazumder for training us with great vigor and sharing with us invaluable experiences and technical expertise. We would also thank the wonderful and extremely cooperative Research Fellows who took the pain of helping us out in-spite of their hectic schedule. And definitely we thank the **Entrepreneurship Development Cell**, of **St. Xavier's College** who had instigated this wonderful Training Program.

We consider this Program to be of great success, as it has proved to be beneficial to us students who had the opportunity to be exposed to real life Research. Professional training of some of the most advanced techniques like Western Blot and PCR and instrument handling like HPLC is really useful to us. The only grief if any would be the time duration, which was quite limited and may be extended for future program.

Thanking you
Yours Sincerely

Krishna Ghosh
Shibo Prasad Mondal
Dhrubajyoti Mishra
Gourab Chatterjee
Rumi? Banerjee
Sanchita Das
Sounitta Choudhuri
Paulami Pal
Priyanka Mukherjee

DATE: 14.03.08
PLACE - Kolkata

Annex 51

Dear Sir,

Great opportunities come to all
but most people
do not know they have met them
for opportunities do not come
with their values
stamped upon them
Each day dawns quite like
other days, in it a single hour
comes quite like the other hours,
but in that day and in that hour
the chance of lifetime faces us.
Thankyou EDC, for
giving me great opportunities
and helping me face every
opportunity of life,
thoughtfully and earnestly
as they come.

With warm regard
Swati

1 Organic Dye Training

2 Organic Compost

3 At GTZ Munich

4 Binghamtom invlted by Prof M Chatterji

5.Google HQ

6 Bee keeping community

7 Intel SFO

8 IITB

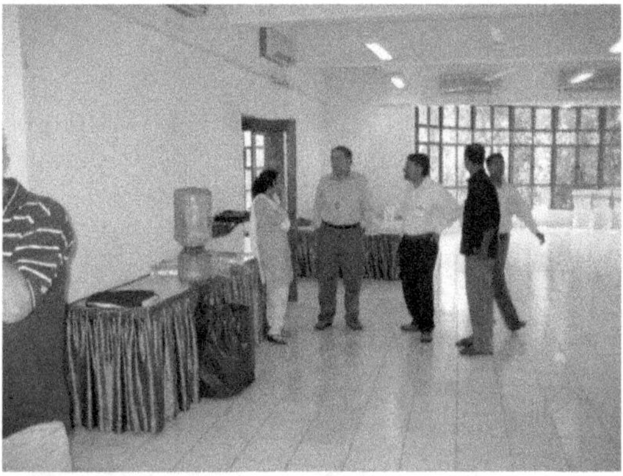

9 Marketing Mantra IITB

10 Mentoring Session

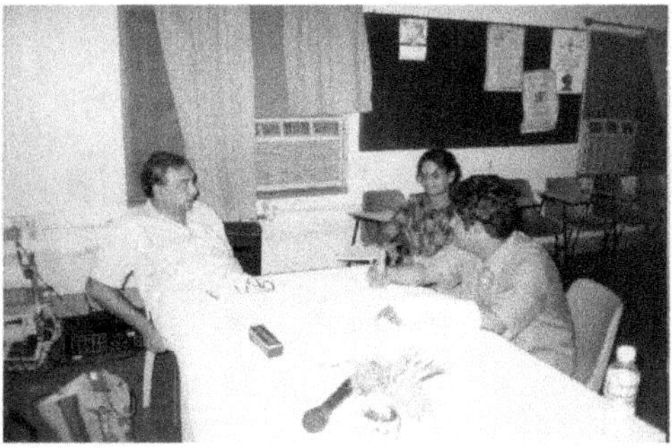

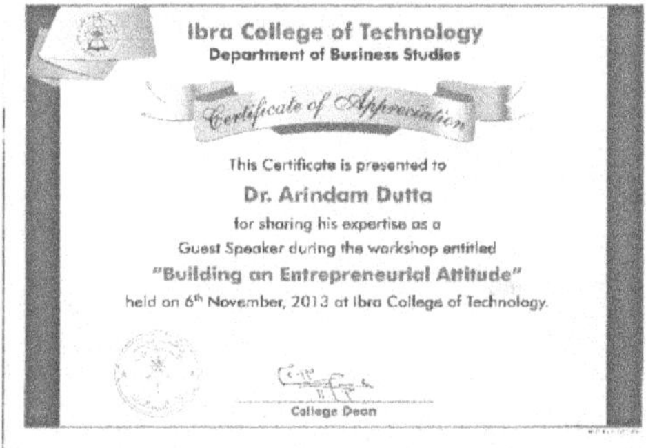

Ibra College of Technology
Department of Business Studies

Certificate of Appreciation

This Certificate is presented to

Dr. Arindam Dutta

for sharing his expertise as a
Guest Speaker during the workshop entitled
"Building an Entrepreneurial Attitude"
held on 6th November, 2013 at Ibra College of Technology.

College Dean

Creating the Entrepreneurial Eco-System

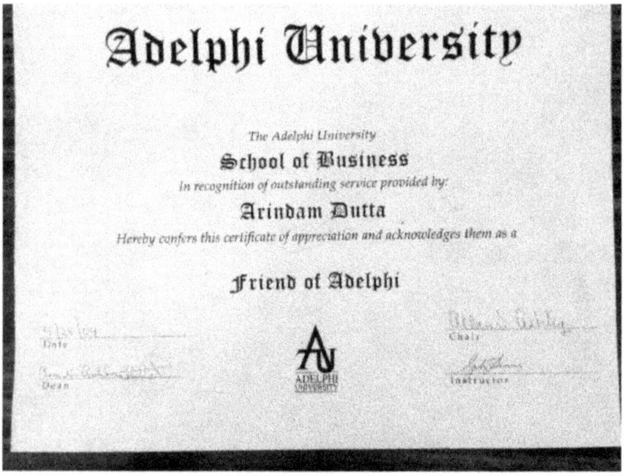
Adelphi University
The Adelphi University
School of Business
In recognition of outstanding service provided by:
Arindam Dutta
Hereby confers this certificate of appreciation and acknowledges them as a
Friend of Adelphi
Chair
Dean
Instructor
ADELPHI UNIVERSITY

Intel+ UC Berkeley Technology Entrepreneurship Education
intel
University of California
Berkeley
Haas School of Business
@Berkeley
This is to Certify That
Arindam Dutta
Successfully Participated in the
Global Faculty Colloquium
November 5-16, 2007

www.ingramcontent.com/pod-product-compliance
Lightning Source LLC
Chambersburg PA
CBHW051450170526
45166CB00001B/182